"We live in a world where profession[...] by personal and work-related obligat[...], and social stress. David Rice shows us how to break free from the confines of self-doubt and a mundane existence to pursue inner peace and satisfaction. This book will have you realizing that your dreams don't have to live in your imagination; they can be your reality!"

—DR. PAMELA MARAGLIANO-MUNIZ
CHIEF EDITOR OF *DENTAL ECONOMICS*

"Good leaders provide direction, purpose, and reason for a group or organization to follow. Great leaders do this with empathy—sharing their knowledge, wisdom, and experience and serving to inspire those around them. I've known David Rice for more than a decade and it's amazing to see his passion for dentistry, his ability to inspire others, and his drive for professional growth now fueling his personal dreams. This book distills a philosophy I've seen him live by, and I hope it can inspire you to make the changes you need to realize your personal dreams, however they may evolve."

—SARAH ANDERS
HU-FRIEDY GROUP VICE PRESIDENT,
NA DENTAL SALES

"David Rice's book came into my life at a time when I needed the right wakeup call! As a young leader, I've devoted so much of my time, energy, and life toward making sure that I do the right thing for my team and career, so much so that I forgot about myself. The introduction alone threw me into a spiral of asking myself, What does my perfect day look like? At the time of writing this, I still don't have an answer. However, I've been super in-tune with the several comfortably uncomfortable moments that are helping me shape my perfect day and ultimately the perfect vision.

"Since I've met him, David has been an aspiring success story. Whether you've met him or not, the thought-provoking questions in this book will help you design your own blueprint. Good luck!"

—HUMAM ALMUKHTAR
MBA AND HEAD OF GLOBAL DIGITAL MARKETING

"David has the unique ability to link hard-to-understand concepts but get you to grasp them almost instantly. His ability to help young professionals connect the dots toward business ownership throughout the years is clearly demonstrated in this book. I'm excited to see how the future of dentistry and beyond embraces these pages, and I hope that they start applying it to their everyday lives and in their pursuit of business ownership. In the end the reader will have a clear strategy for how to get the things done that are most important to them."

—JONATHAN MILLER
BUSINESS START-UP SPECIALIST

"From the very start, David's honest words are compelling and thought provoking. His own experiences, success, and failure are relatable, and his wisdom is incredibly powerful. The strategies in this book are essential for any business owner trying to define success and happiness for themselves, especially as they navigate the evolving postpandemic world."

—TERESA DENIKE
CEO, SLEEP BETTER NYC

IS EVERYONE
SMILING
BUT YOU?

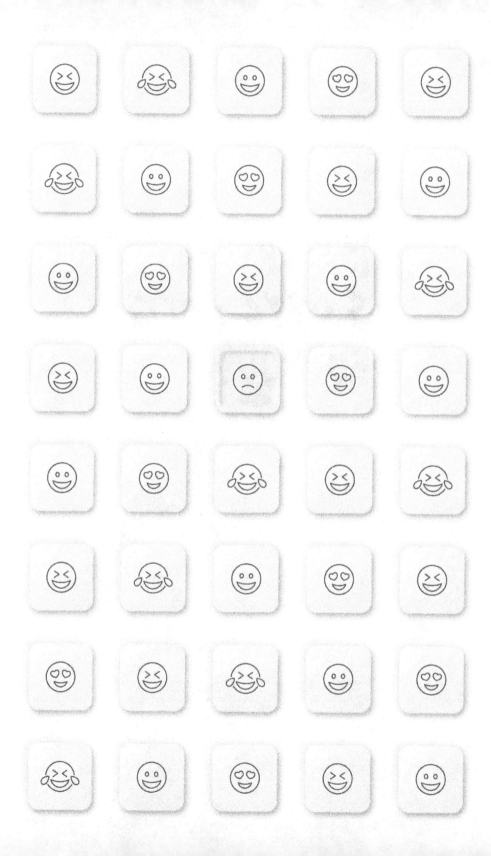

IS EVERYONE
SMILING
BUT YOU?

LEVEL UP YOUR LIFE PRACTICE NOW

DAVID RICE

Advantage | Books

Published by Advantage, Charleston, South Carolina.
Member of Advantage Media.

ADVANTAGE is a registered trademark, and the Advantage colophon is a trademark of Advantage Media Group, Inc.

Printed in the United States of America.

10 9 8 7 6 5 4 3 2 1

ISBN: 978-1-64225-375-7 (Paperback)
ISBN: 978-1-64225-458-7 (eBook)

Library of Congress Control Number: 2023902189

Cover design by Analisa Smith.
Layout design by Lance Buckley.

Advantage Media helps busy entrepreneurs, CEOs, and leaders write and publish a book to grow their business and become the authority in their field. Advantage authors comprise an exclusive community of industry professionals, idea-makers, and thought leaders. Do you have a book idea or manuscript for consideration? We would love to hear from you at **AdvantageMedia.com**.

For Anastasia, who ignites my soul every day

CONTENTS

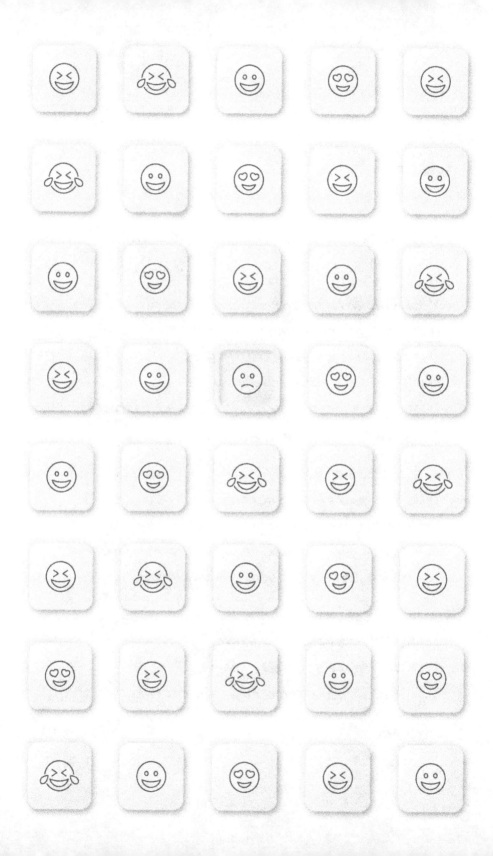

ACKNOWLEDGMENTS

I remember as a little kid, usually after losing a baseball game, my mom or dad would share a lesson I'm guessing you've heard: it's not whether you win or lose—it's how you play the game. It was a lesson lost on me until later in life when I realized *how* I played the game and *who* I played it with determined the win or loss.

Every lesson in this book is a reflection of my wins, losses, and, most importantly, the people who've had an incredible impact on my life.

To Anastasia, words could never express the love and inspiration I feel with, from, and for you. Every time you smile, I remember every reason why how I play the game matters and every reason why a losing moment is simply a challenge we will overcome together. Morning coffee, walks on the bay with Gibbs Rice, silly laughs, our own sillier vocabulary, crime shows on the cuddle couch, and more—you are truly my partner in crime.

To my mom and dad who believed in me even when I didn't believe in myself. You've taught and continue to teach me who I want to be when I grow up. Most amazingly, you do it by example rather than mere words. Thank you for that.

To my sister, Jennifer; her hubby, Jason; and Alyssa, Leah, and Josh. Who you are and what you do every day blow me away. You are each an example of who everyone should strive to be.

To Mark and the East Amherst team, for your undying patience, kindness, and love. There will never be enough words to thank you.

Last and certainly not least, to my team at Ignite. Building better for so many with your hard work is literally my dream come alive. Together, *we rise!*

INTRODUCTION

*When the wind of change blows, some people
build walls, others build windmills.*

—CHINESE PROVERB

Are you happy? Be honest with yourself.

We all face obstacles. Life ebbs and flows. There are times when things fire on all cylinders, and then we hit a wall. It could be a physical wall or something deeper. Often it's a *perceived* wall, and we get stuck. There's a choice to make. It's important to see life this way—that you have a choice. We can choose to stay stuck, which inevitably means going backward, or decide to dive into the unknown.

You're either growing or shrinking in life—succeeding or dying. If this seems harsh, understand we won't be pulling any punches here.

It's hard to grasp that you have complete agency over your future, but it's even harder to suffer in a life that eats away at you. Listen, making choices won't come easy. It won't even give you fast results. Everyone will have a different trajectory, but the first step is deciding that you want to feel better about yourself. The second step is *working* on the principles you're about to learn—truly incorporating them to see results. I'll give you the tools for doing just that.

Once you've decided to create change in your life, your outcomes depend upon how you *proceed* with that decision. If you have this book in your hand, you've already realized, *I need to do something.* If you're ready to take action, this is the right book for you. If you haven't reached this conclusion, you might want to put this book down until you're ready. Save it until the discomfort of being unhappy propels you to change it all.

I'm the founder of IgniteDDS, the largest community of young dentists and dental students in our nation. I'm also a public speaker and teacher. Today, I wake up with a passion for what I do, but this didn't happen overnight, and it wasn't the original vision for my life. In fact, I wasn't living with much vision at all in my successful dental practice. I was doing what I thought I was supposed to be doing.

To the outside eye, life was going well in my New York practice, but I hit obstacles, just as I'm sure you have—some of them were my own doing, and others were expected life challenges. I knew I had choices, but I stayed where I was for a long time, even though something was missing. There was an emptiness inside. One day I woke up and couldn't do it anymore—I had to make a choice. There were possibilities out there, and I imagined my potential. I looked at what others were accomplishing and embraced my current mantra: "Why not *me?*" The purpose of sharing all this is to ask, "Why not *you?*"

Keep asking these questions every step of the way: *Why not me? Why not now?*

I had to make difficult decisions to step out of a career that appeared amazing but inwardly was killing me. I don't say that lightly. I'd lost the joy of waking up each day. I worked with colleagues and patients I cared for, but I'd forgotten my fire. Sundays became awful because I knew Monday was next, and I was living for the weekend— for a day off. I was living for just about anything but my job.

In reality, we spend our brief lives on this planet in our professional routines, rather than our personal dreams. It wasn't working for me. I knew I needed to make a change and embrace the fact that I could achieve larger goals. My evolution came down to asking *who* I wanted in my life, *what* I wanted to be doing, and *why* it was fundamental to make difficult adjustments. Ultimately, this led to a new location, my lovely wife, Anastasia, and forming IgniteDDS. Yes, all these things make me smile.

I had to walk myself through this entire process. I've lived every lesson in this book and refined, tweaked, refined, and tweaked them again. If you're anything like me, you need a map for this journey, and I've spent my life creating it. You may feel like you have nowhere to go or no one to turn to. The truth is that this world is wide open when you follow the right actionable steps—when you know what to shoot for. This process is life changing and utterly unique to your big picture—these lessons apply to *your* vision.

I'll walk you through the process of defining a vision for yourself—not what society or family have told you to do. Then you can lean into personal investment and risk. You'll be rearranging your time and resources to create what you want, instead of staying on the path that is chipping away at you. There's a good chance your rote routine has blinded you to your potential.

What's the number one reason people avoid change? They're afraid of discomfort. I ask, "Are you uncomfortable enough today to do something uncomfortable?" Yes, change ushers in some immediate pain, but imagine how uncomfortable life will be if you stay still. We were born to change—to lean into the unknown and create happiness for ourselves. There are two kinds of stress: distress and eustress. Research shows, "Working and living outside of our comfort zone is a good thing. It's when we feel overwhelmed that stress can turn negative. That's what makes eustress such an important part of our overall health."[1]

In an article from Healthline, Dr. Casey Lee, MA, notes that negative stress "can lead to anxiety, depression, and a decrease in performance." At the same time, "eustress produces positive feelings of excitement, fulfillment, meaning, satisfaction, and well-being." The takeaway proves that eustress "is good because you feel confident, adequate, and stimulated by the challenge you experience from the stressor."

According to Bronnie Ware, best known for her studies on deathbed regrets, here are the top five:[2]

1. *I WISH I'D HAD THE COURAGE TO LIVE A LIFE TRUE TO MYSELF, NOT THE LIFE OTHERS EXPECTED OF ME.*

2. *I WISH I HADN'T WORKED SO HARD.*

3. *I WISH I'D HAD THE COURAGE TO EXPRESS MY FEELINGS.*

4. *I WISH I HAD STAYED IN TOUCH WITH MY FRIENDS.*

5. *I WISH THAT I HAD LET MYSELF BE HAPPIER.*

I always consider the emotions of people who reach the end of their lives and feel regret. As Ware's list shows, we all regret similar things. I want you to imagine what life will feel like five, ten, or fifty

---

1   Sara Lindberg, "Eustress: The Good Stress," Healthline, January 2019, **https://www. healthline.com/health/eustress#good-stress.**

2   Kathy Caprino, "The Top Regrets of the Dying and What We Need to Learn from Them," *Forbes*, December 2019, https://www.forbes.com/sites/kathycaprino/2019/12/13/the-top-regrets-of-the-dying-and-what-we-need-to-learn-from-them/?sh=243366287ce7.

years from now if you don't go for it. Change gets harder as life carries on. With habit, you get more stuck.

I visualize this in reverse. How would David Rice be doing right now if he'd never strived for his dream? Well, his personal and professional lives would have suffered drastically. The people around him who sensed something was off would've grown tired of the person who hadn't taken action. He would be angry, upset, and short-tempered—frustrated all the time. Essentially, I would be devoid of the joy I feel each day.

When you get lost in something you love in a positive way, every relationship you have improves because you aren't faking it. You're living your dream. You can't pretend to be happy every day! I did until I couldn't anymore. The fantastic team at my practice that I worked so hard to build would've disappeared. My great relationships with family would've gone away. My personal relationship with Anastasia perhaps never would have happened. You know, people can only tolerate so much. Choosing to be happier lifts up those around you. This path isn't entirely selfish. Everyone benefits.

Ask yourself, "What am I willing to sacrifice today to have a better tomorrow?" Because better tomorrows just build upon better tomorrows.

This work is for young people looking to craft their futures or anyone who, like me, woke up one day and thought something had to change. I meet so many people who have no sense of their potential.

> ASK YOURSELF, "WHAT AM I WILLING TO SACRIFICE TODAY TO HAVE A BETTER TOMORROW?" BECAUSE BETTER TOMORROWS JUST BUILD UPON BETTER TOMORROWS.

They think everyone out there is better than they. When they see somebody achieving new heights, they believe others have innate skill sets: "They must be different from me. They're smarter. They were privileged because of where they came from or opportunities that fell into their laps."

My friends, this is garbage. It just is! *You* have the potential to build the life of your dreams. In your hands, at this moment, you have the ingredients. I'm not here to define success for you, but I promise you can attain that unique vision for yourself—whatever your definition might be. It's silly that we assume only a small percentage of the population achieves their goals. (Well, it's true but unnecessary.) You can intentionally build your future. As you'll discover, so much of this process is about stepping out of your box—reaching out to others, putting in the work, and educating yourself.

Be radically honest with yourself. Have a look in the mirror. The only person holding you back is the image you see. If you're willing to put in the work to go from where you're at to your dreams—if you're willing to take these steps—it's all possible. Table this book if you're not ready, but if you are, let's begin a new approach to life—achieving what you want.

Following each chapter, there will be a blog and corresponding video on my website that continues the discussion. You'll find all this and more at drdavidrice.com/resources. For a faster option, use the QR code at the back of this book.

- Write down the answer to this question: "What's one thing you dream of achieving that you think is impossible?"

_____

_____

_____

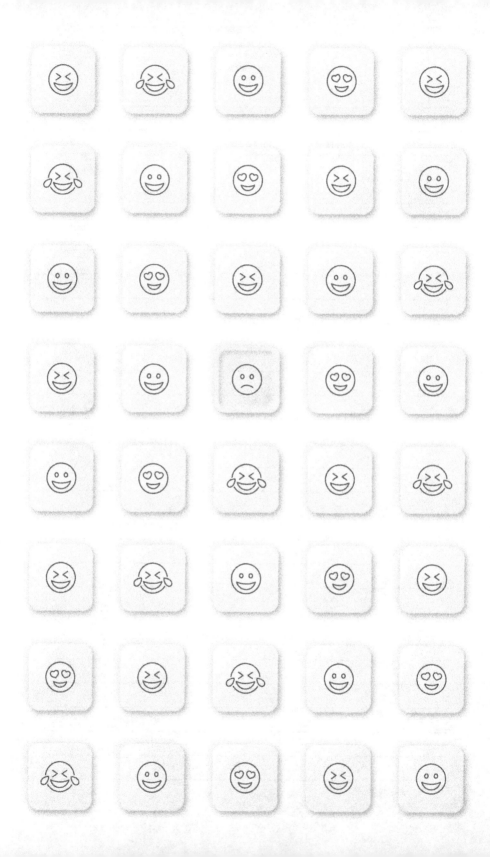

PART I

LIVING WITH INTENT

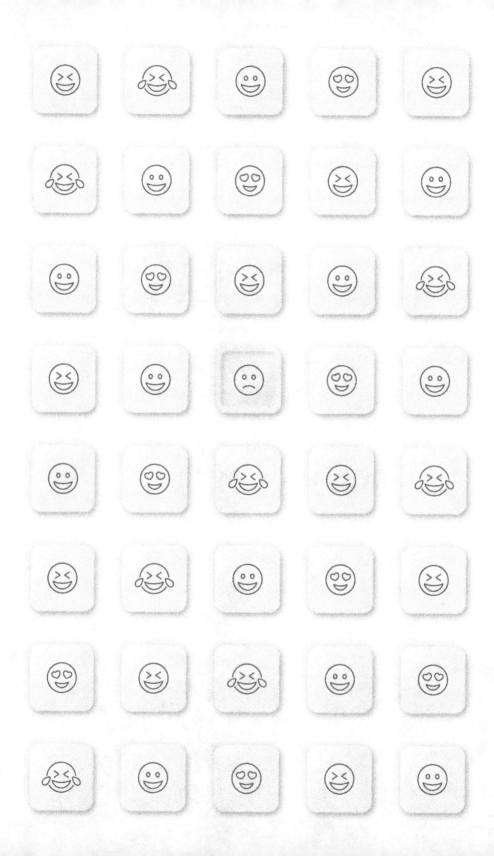

CHAPTER ONE

DESIGN YOUR PERFECT DAY

Every day can look like your ideal day if you do something ideal.

—RICHIE NORTON

I spent a lot of time in my formative years doing what I was supposed to do. I took the straight and narrow path—staying in my hometown of Buffalo, New York, to be close to family while thriving in my dental career. I was a success, living a life that was grounded and sustainable.

There was only one problem—it wasn't.

I recall a low point when I looked in the mirror and said, "I don't want to do this anymore." I'd ignored this inner voice for a long time. I was a yes person. A people pleaser. And listen, I loved relationships, but I knew it was time to finally please *myself* along the way.

When it comes to designing your perfect day, I'm referring to both personal and professional success. On paper—in our modern age, on social media—you can be living a life that anyone would deem perfect, but if you're not aligned with what makes you happy—your *where*, *what*, and *why*—you'll never achieve your potential. If you feel the same as I did all those years ago, it's okay. Look in the mirror, forgive yourself, figure out what you want, and build better. Learn from your discomfort to create the life you want. That's what this book is about.

Today, most of my success doesn't come from what I did right—it comes from what I did wrong. I knew the perfect day for me was waking up near water. I'm a sunshine guy, a water guy. It's where I felt most at peace and where I knew I'd thrive, but I ignored this. At the time, the priority was being close to family because that's what I was *supposed* to do. That was the right thing to do. One day, I just woke up. Tragedy helped me to embrace a new direction.

In my practice, I had a young dentist who worked for me, an associate named Mark. He was talented and hardworking and quickly advanced to become a partner. He was a personable guy with a bright future. Tragically, he lost his wife, who was only twenty-seven years old. She died a week after they'd welcomed their firstborn child. I'd never witnessed tragedy on that level, and my thought was this: *You know what? I don't want to live for somebody else one more day. Life is too short.*

That was my *aha* moment. I knew I needed to stop pressuring myself to do what others wanted. At that point, I didn't decide to jump ship on everything in life, but I did choose to start figuring out what mattered to *me*. It became clear that no one knows what's going to happen tomorrow. In reality, we have no idea. And here was this young guy—new house, new baby—and life was just coming together by everyone's definition of how life was *supposed* to come together. All of a sudden, his world was turned upside down.

It had never occurred to me to design a perfect day because that day would take place thousands of miles away. Water was the only clear direction, so I ventured twenty minutes out to Lake Erie to gain some perspective. Hey, it was a start and a location I could quickly find. I'll never forget sitting on this enormous rock, looking out over the lake, and feeling a sense of peace. My mind removed the clutter of the day-to-day. I didn't have my cell phone with me. No one could get ahold of me. I wasn't distracted by work, family, or friends. It was my time to figure out who I wanted to be when I grew up. In a very structured way, I began laying out what my perfect day might look like at home and work—how much personal time I wanted and how I would balance out a life that had no balance.

This realization was nearly two decades ago. The moment changed my life forever.

I asked the chairman of the dental school where I was teaching for a leave of absence. My grieving associate needed time to heal, and my goal was to work two extra days in my practice so I could pay Mark to stay home as long as it took. After not being granted the leave of absence, I pulled the keys out of my pocket, handed them over, and said, "I quit. Some things are more important."

Leaving my teaching position was another *aha* moment because I ended up missing it. I wanted to continue working with dental students. I was interviewed by a dental magazine regarding my consulting work that helped other dental practices to succeed. It's weird how life works sometimes. In the discussion, I brought up teaching students and young dentists, and the guy who interviewed me said, "Wait a second. Hold the interview. You've got to figure out how to embrace your passion for teaching young dentists while creating a business out of it."

Life and timing.

The very next week, I was a guest speaker at the dental school I'd resigned from. I returned with great intention, then waited for students to approach me at the end of my lecture. When they did, rather than answering all their questions, I offered, "Hey, let's have lunch." That lunch became a dinner party for ten students, and then that dinner evolved into twenty students. Eventually, it turned into a dinner for three hundred students over the course of the entire semester. These interactions led to the formation of IgniteDDS. My passion for teaching and dentistry became my business. The mission for Ignite was, and still is, simple and attuned with my deeper goals—to educate, encourage, and empower both dental students and practicing dentists.

Living my perfect day is a reality now because I'm living my passion, which can be a reality for you too. Know what your goal is, figure out who you need in your life to help build it, then plan on how to make the dream come to life. There's always a way, and it's just a matter of design and determination. When attaining the life you want, failure is not an option. Quitting is not an option. Getting where you want to be requires conviction. Designing your life, switching gears—these are possible at any age. It's never too late.

> KNOW WHAT YOUR GOAL IS, FIGURE OUT WHO YOU NEED IN YOUR LIFE TO HELP BUILD IT, THEN PLAN ON HOW TO MAKE THE DREAM COME TO LIFE.

It might surprise you, but I hate being organized. I don't always like the details of life. I'm inherently a big-picture, throw-paint-at-the-wall, larger-vision kind of guy. Thanks to this, I've learned how to achieve my perfect day—I've learned how to organize that big vision in a way that keeps me focused. Everyone can create their ideal life, but there's so much distraction. We get bogged down by the *shoulds* and miss what makes us happy—we lose sight of our authentic goals and values. When you have a clear vision for your future, it can boil down to your perfect day. Sound too simple? It's truly not. It's already inside of you.

Your perfect day might seem unattainable because you have too many obligations. The very idea of a perfect day perhaps frustrates you, as you're living in survival mode. Maybe you can't even visualize it. This process will look different for everyone, but at the heart of it, these ideas will guide you to where you want to be, what you want to be doing, and why this even matters.

First up, let's take a look at your happy place.

WHERE DO YOU WANT TO BE?

You will recognize your own path when you come upon it, because you will suddenly have all the energy and imagination you will ever need.

—JERRY GILLIES

Think big picture.

Changing my location was the first step in embracing my core self, and my life opened up after that. My career shifted, and my focus shifted—I was moving toward many perfect days in the long term.

I guarantee you that everyone, at some point, is going to feel stuck. We all go down paths that weren't well thought out. Just as isolating—directions that were well thought out but unsustainable. None of these roads led you astray. They got you closer to your dreams. But let's begin with the present moment. While you read this book, how do your surroundings make you feel? If you're excited for today and tomorrow, great! You're in the right place. If you're not at ease, it's time for introspection. And take a breath.

I shared my experience at Lake Erie because *location* changed the course of my life for the better. My vision for myself opened up after I leaned into a fundamental need inside of me. I wanted to be by the water, under the bright sunshine, and living a life with breathing space. Everyone's location is going to be different. Go back in your memory. What was that moment in time when you were blissful? Where were you, and who surrounded you? That happiness doesn't need to be limited to your vacation in Cancun three years ago, but if that's the case, it's a clue for you.

Many obstacles get in the way of us using intuition to seek happiness. There's pressure from parents and friends—no matter your age. It seems impossible to escape from our ingrained habits. We're all bound by our past experiences and the experiences of those around us. Recently, I returned to my hometown and started having conversations with people I'd grown up with and had known for thirty years. The predominant discussion sounded like this: "We all walked the same path because of how we grew up and what our parents taught us."

This trend isn't wrong. It's tradition. But tradition can inhibit your big picture.

Dan Sullivan's book *Who Not How*[3] references Dr. Robert Kegan's definition of the *socializing self:* "When a person operates out of fear, anxiety, and dependence." He then highlights the *transforming self:* "The highest form of psychological and emotional evolution." My and my friends' limited experiences were due to a core group of people in our lives—wonderful people who shared the viewpoint of Kegan's *socializing self.* When you open up to new experiences, you expand your self-knowledge. You get to choose *where* you want to be. I didn't realize this until I left Buffalo.

---

3   Dan Sullivan and Dr. Benjamin Hardy, *Who Not How: The Formula to Achieve Bigger Goals through Accelerating Teamwork* (California: Hay House Business, 2020).

While growing up, studying to be a dentist seemed like a sound choice, and I had a passion for it. My guidance counselors and parents promoted this path for obvious reasons. No matter your age, people get locked into solid jobs, or even not-so-solid jobs, because the money is consistent and gives a sense of *safety*. Pardon me, but "safety is a fence, and fences are for sheep." Boundaries lead to discovery, and discovery kicks fear and pressure to the curb. And trust me, you'll need to develop boundaries to push out of your status quo. Stepping out of your comfort zone proves you have nothing to lose and much to gain.

So how do you dream bigger and get to your happy place? Tap into those moments when you were at peace and your creativity soared. Hold onto these memories as fundamental information that is part of your big picture—a big picture that informs your perfect day. Your *where* is unique to you—water, mountains, desert, or a foreign country. A specific town or state. A big city or a small town. A large house or a tiny cabin by a lake. So why don't you currently live in a place where you feel whole? Being in the wrong place is common for a lot of people. It's "normal" not to follow your intuition about where you should be. You have obligations, that tried-and-true job you've held for years, or your parents have been pushing you to be. Perhaps you're an adult who went down the lawyer/doctor/dentist/*anything* path, but you haven't been happy.

Listen, these are all great jobs. I should know! But if you're not in the right location, the most solid of jobs will not hold. You're suffering inside. What's your big picture location? It's the best place to start, even when you're nickel-and-diming it.

- Below, write three places *where* you felt most like yourself—you had a sharp mind, felt creative, and sensed that breathing space.

_____

_____

_____

WHAT DO YOU WANT TO DO?

Everybody wants to be a bodybuilder, but nobody wants to lift no heavy-ass weights.

—RONNIE COLEMAN

I love exercising every morning, which was part of my vision for my perfect day. I neglected things like this when I was practicing dentistry full time. If you're a young professional, I strongly advise you to visualize your *where* and *what* before you get bogged down. If you already have a substantial career but the balance is off, take steps to incorporate more of *what* you want to be doing to achieve your fundamental goals in life. Don't let the daily minutiae override the big picture.

Do you see yourself exercising every morning, walking your dog, hanging out with your kids, or meditating? Do you smile when you think of more quiet evenings with your spouse, or more evenings with a family member or pet? How do these activities fit in with the daily tasks of your career, and more importantly, how do you prevent your career from taking over elements of your perfect day? Your perfect day must provide time for you to be in your zone, whatever that looks like for you—music, art, relationships. You might be asking yourself, but isn't this a book about career success? It is. But a perfect day that nurtures all aspects of yourself will lead to more far-reaching success. It's guaranteed. As a young professional, these activities should come first. As a mature professional who needs to pivot, these priorities will take you where you need to be.

When you boil it down, your day is about habits. These habits can be moving you forward, keeping you in the same place, or backtracking you. My routine used to be survival oriented: get up, go into the office, deal with patients on a case-by-case basis, and then return home and see what the evening brings. This was the pattern I thought I had to adhere to, but I see now that I wasn't directing my habits toward my big picture goals. I was going nowhere.

Your habits aren't something you walk into. They're something you choose and expand. In the next chapter, we'll delve into what you're *genuinely* hoping to achieve in life, but for now, understand that habits aren't just about what time you shower and what you eat for breakfast. Habits are ingrained choices that you make about how to spend your time. Your habits ultimately become your priorities. Your priorities become your perfect day.

For a bit of fun, let's look at the *Autobiography of Benjamin Franklin*. Franklin was a genius when it came to productivity. As a man who wore many hats, including entrepreneur, politician, writer, scientist, and inventor, his daily routine was his perfect day. Franklin was a wise man indeed.

- 5:00–7:00 a.m.–Rise, wash, and address powerful goodness! Contrive the day's business and take the resolution of the day; prosecute the present study and breakfast.
- 8:00–11:00 a.m.–Work.
- 12:00–1:00 p.m.–Read or overlook my accounts and dine.
- 2:00–5:00 p.m.–Work.
- 6:00–9:00 p.m.–Put things in their places, supper, music or diversion, or conversation; examination of the day.
- 10:00 p.m. to 4:00 a.m.–Sleep.

Franklin's was a life balanced by productivity, personal enjoyment, and introspection. These were his habits, but what exactly are habits? According to the *Oxford Dictionary*, a habit is "a settled or regular tendency or practice, especially one that is hard to give up." There are positive and negative habits, but when designing your perfect day, you should focus on practices that inevitably move you to your larger goals. Do you feel confused about which habits to strengthen? You shouldn't be. In Donald Miller's book *Business Made Simple*,[4] he states, "A value-driven individual does not choose to be confused."

You know when habits aren't serving you—when people surrounding you aren't moving you forward. We call this *confusion* when we're afraid to take action. Please don't allow yourself to be confused when creating habits that align with your big picture. There's a good chance you're not confused. You're just scared to do something about it. I would often get confused early on because my life didn't feel right. I wasn't in the right place, and my daily routine wasn't taking me where I wanted to be. Having a vision will help you see which habits might have you stuck.

Or which location has you stuck.

With a bit of introspection, your *where* starts to form, *what* you want to do each day becomes clear, and you find yourself on a path to your perfect day, putting you on a fast or slow track to your goals. Yes, fast or slow. We're all going to run this race at a different pace—some are sprinters, and others are marathoners. The key is to know *your* race, because if you're a marathon runner and you sprint, you'll tire out and quit. If you're a sprinter and I make you run a marathon, you'll be so bored and won't finish.

---

4   Donald Miller, *Business Made Simple: 60 Days to Master Leadership, Sales, Marketing, Execution, Management, Personal Productivity and More* (New York: HarperCollins).

Understand how fast you want to get to your *what*—one day at a time. Start small if you have to. My perfect day didn't come overnight, and changing my habits didn't happen overnight. But my big picture compelled me to do it all.

- Write three to five *what* items—things you envision yourself doing daily to reach your goals. Later in the book, we'll discuss building the right habits, but for now, let your imagination run with it.

_____

_____

_____

_____

_____

_____

_____

_____

_____

WHY HAVE A PERFECT DAY?

The hardest part of any important task is getting started on it in the first place. Once you actually begin work on a valuable task, you seem to be naturally motivated to continue.

—BRIAN TRACY

I'm talking about *why* last, but my *why* came before *where* and *what*. It seems funny to ask why someone should have a perfect day, but if you need to make profound changes, then discovering your new direction will mean letting go of things and even pissing some people off. So be it.

I'm not a "Fake it till you make it" kind of guy. If you're unhappy at home or work for whatever reason, there's no way to hide it for long. The house of cards will crash at some point, even if it only crashes internally. If the business house of cards doesn't crash at first, a crash in your personal house of cards will pull it all down. This realization was my *why* moment—again, that *aha*. The only sustainable choice was to find my happy spot while having a perfect day aligned with my long-term goals. Being a dentist wasn't enough. I wanted happiness, missed teaching, and craved freedom from the four walls closing in on me—freedom from being stuck in an office all day. I wanted a team around me that could help me nurture my goals. Once you feel how fundamental these big picture aspects are, I know you'll understand.

I use a blocking method for my perfect day, fueled by a deeper understanding of myself and what is meaningful for me. I use my iPhone for this, but you can download the PDF from my website. In the search bar, type in "Perfect Day PDF." The goal is to have your blocks fuel you as much as mine fuel me. My *why* is the catalyst for every aspect of my scheduling. Here is how a typical day looks. Take it only as an example.

6 AM	Workout
7 AM	Family. Morning walk 3-4 miles. Breakfast. Shower.
8 AM	Emails, Social Media Check In
9 AM	Meeting opportunities
10 AM	Video Concept/Script writing
11 AM	
Noon	
1 PM	Lunch / Video Shoot
2 PM	
3 PM	
4 PM	Meeting opportunities
5 PM	

Even though my schedule aspires to Benjamin Franklin–like precision, I create a buffer for myself. If anything takes longer than anticipated, there's built-in time for that. Something might happen, so I schedule a gap. I try to predict the week as best as I can—a year in advance. You heard that right.

Scheduling a whole year seems impossible, but it isn't. I know where my speaking engagements will be, the vacations I'll be taking, and anything else relating to my work and social life. If something needs to change within a day or a week, all the blocks still matter, so I find a place for those blocks when things shift. I stay on track and get things done that I know are necessary. You'll learn much more about this when we get to the bucket method in chapter 2.

My time blocks wouldn't be complete without blocked time with my beloved wife, Anastasia. When my life was all dentistry, personal time was never possible. These days, it's the priority. I've discovered my *where*, I've chosen my *what*, and now the real focus is on quality time with those I love while achieving professional goals. Don't overlook the power of personal priorities and how they only enhance your professional success in the end.

My blocks show that at 6:30 p.m., the phone goes off for the rest of the night. Sure, if my parents were to call due to an emergency, I'd pick that up. If there's an evening obligation once a month, that's fine, and it's put on the schedule. But evenings are devoted to personal time with Anastasia—the time block I'm most proud of. So what does blocking facilitate?

Expectations and boundaries.

I can't stress enough how important it is to create the life of your dreams by releasing obligations and pressures. Boundaries terrify most people, so set expectations instead. Life is short, and if you're not spending a reasonable amount of time doing what you cherish, surrounded by those you choose, I promise you'll have regrets. Benjamin Franklin knew this.

Again, everyone is different. If you're a night owl and like to work into the late hours, create your personal time blocks in the day. If you work from home, pick your day—or several days—to devote to personal time. Remember, knowing and honoring yourself only increases success. Don't be afraid to say no, especially when so much can swallow your time and energy. Your time, work, and *connections* are priceless. Make your choices and build the habits that align with your big picture, day after day.

We're about to cover a lot. Can you implement all of these concepts and strategies today? No. In my teaching across the country, I always bring up being a Buffalo kid and seeing things as *pizza by the slice or the whole pie*. The concept goes like this: I'm a whole pie guy. I need the big picture, which helps me visualize where I'm going and organize my time. But you can't have the whole pie unless you take it slice by slice. Within our pizza analogy—what's not to like?—see the whole pie, and then go slice by slice.

It took me years to craft my perfect day, and maybe you need to start with one perfect day this week. Throw it at the wall and see if it sticks. If it doesn't, keep imagining and start again. Say you found your perfect day, but you don't know how to make it sustainable *every* day. Start with one perfect day, then two, one week, then one month. Sooner than you think, you'll be propelled toward what *you* want—your ideal life.

Don't measure yourself against me. My way isn't better. It's just the way that works for me, and as you're on this journey to self-discovery and releasing pressures that don't serve you, I promise you'll discover your way. We can all get to where we want to go, but we each do it a little differently—fueled by *where*, *what*, and *why*. As you implement my concepts and strategies, you'll find yourself reaching the *aha* moment that takes you to your perfect day, every day. Chapter 2 will give you further insight into your *why* by exploring your core values.

Essentially, these values are why you're here. You know you need a change.

- Go back to your *what* list and give each of those habits a *why*. Put intention behind what it is you want to accomplish.

TAKEAWAYS

- Location is the foundation of wellness, productivity, and personal growth.
- Your perfect day starts with *where*, which leads to *what*, and is fueled by *why*.
- Boundaries lead to personal growth and understanding.
- Block out your perfect day using the scheduling sheet on my website or on your phone.
- Head over to my website at drdavidrice.com/resources for my blog, "The Value of Designing Your Perfect Day," and enjoy the corresponding video. For a faster link, use the QR code at the back of this book.

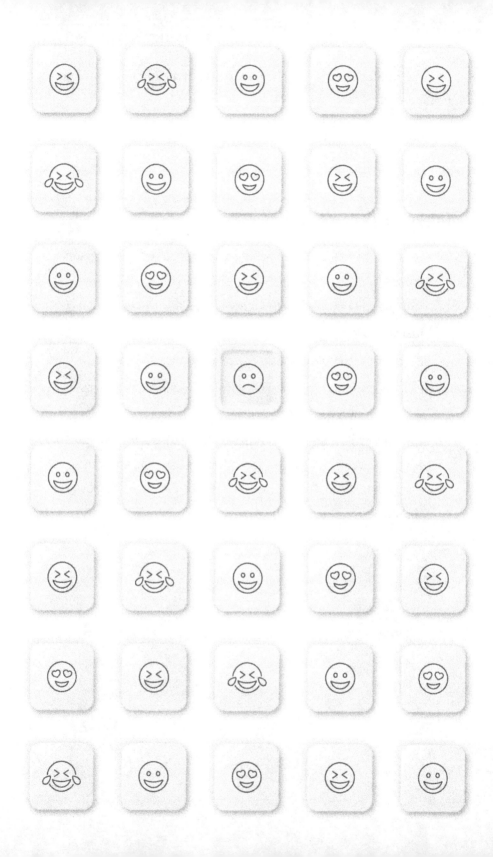

CHAPTER TWO

DESIGN YOUR CORE VALUES

The secret to achieving inner peace lies in understanding our inner core values—those things in our lives that are most important to us—and then seeing that they are reflected in the daily events of our lives.

—HYRUM W. SMITH

My successful cousin decided he wanted to sit on the beach all day, every day, for the rest of his life. He thought this would encompass his core values, and he could afford to do it. So at fifty, he retired, and by fifty-one and a half, he was back working again because he was unfulfilled.

As it turned out, his decision wasn't what he thought it would be. His departure from the beach and return to the office wasn't about money. It wasn't even that he didn't love being on the beach. He lost his balance and wasn't living his core values every day.

I bring this up because sometimes people get confused about their core values or what core values even are. We're going to explore this topic because there's a good chance your *fantasy* life won't be fulfilling. There's so much more to it than that.

My cousin's decision was common. Everyone wants to arrive at the day when they can choose whatever they want to do, but lo and behold, many need their core values to guide them back to a more meaningful existence. So my cousin is doing what he was doing before—albeit a little differently.

Sometimes these full-circle experiences teach us what's most meaningful in life. I didn't move to a location with water so I could stare at it all day—I moved here because I understood that the happiness I feel each morning when I wake up drives me to be my best.

When you know who you are and what's important to you, you don't get lost in the trap of letting go of professional goals to find joy. People strive to accomplish things for a reason. The beauty of my cousin's experience is that we all can course correct.

Like most, you accept what *is* rather than going for what's possible—what you truly want. Life lesson: One day, you're going to need to make that change, but designing it today instead of life designing it for you in your forties, fifties, and beyond is ideal. Ask me how I know. I suppose I'm a poster child for the midlife pivot, but the happiness I feel now could have come sooner. Where would I be now if I'd started earlier?

WHAT ARE CORE VALUES?

Core values are traits or qualities that are not just worthwhile, they represent an individual's or an organization's highest priorities, deeply held beliefs, and core, fundamental driving forces.

—SUSAN M. HEATHFIELD

In the simplest of terms, core values come from that little voice inside that reminds you of what is right and what is wrong—for *you.* Each of us has this voice. These values instruct us *where* we want to be, *what* we want to be doing, and *who* is most valuable. People get off track when, for whatever reason, they stop listening to this voice.

They're tuning it out.

This voice gets overwhelmed by noise because there's either something to do or something we *should* do instead of following our inner guidance. That's why defining core values and designing your time around them is fundamental. The blocking document you downloaded for your perfect day will get a boost now. Every day, you're blocking core values. It takes practice, so use a pencil instead of a pen.

Anything that is big picture for you acts as a lighthouse. It's a beacon. When you've lost your way in a dark ocean and you see that spinning, eclipsing light off in the distance, you've found your way home. Core values not only lead to personal happiness, but they also lead to success. Your goal might be to go out and make a lot of money, but there's a chance this won't mean much at the end of the day. Your home is where your core values live—your happiness lives—and it's where the definition of success lives. You might scratch your head when I say this, but whether you define your success by money, time, comfort, or health, it's easy to achieve these when you stay true to yourself.

Chase just one thing: a better self tomorrow. You'll find yourself unsatisfied when you chase someone else's dreams just because they look or sound good to you. When you chase someone else in general, even if you catch them, you'll find yourself with a new someone else to chase. Perhaps a pursuit isn't aligned with what you believe to be important in life. In that case, all the money in the world, and all the corporate climbing in the world, will be unfulfilling, and you'll find yourself searching and chasing for what's missing—whether that's people or just distraction and filling a hole.

But the hole isn't filled by money, people, or things you can purchase on Amazon. It's filled by being *where* you want to be, doing *what* you want to do, and knowing *why* you're doing this (i.e., your larger vision for your life).

Knowing your values and keeping them in mind can be achieved in different ways. Ultimately, it's best to understand that these beacons will lead to enduring fulfillment and success. Why? Because you have solid ground beneath your feet—a values-driven launching pad. Fulfilling your values only adds to your confidence and well-being, while ignoring these values will deflate you in every way.

> HAVING YOUR CORE VALUES REFLECTED IN YOUR DAILY BLOCKS TAKES TIME AND EXPERIMENTATION, BUT THIS DISCIPLINE WILL PREVENT YOU FROM GETTING LOST IN THE NOISE OF LIFE.

Having your core values reflected in your daily blocks takes time and experimentation, but this discipline will prevent you from getting lost in the noise of life. Many of us wake up and think, *God, I'm super busy today.* That's a terrible feeling! But being busy is different from being *productive.* Productivity aligns with your values, and busyness is just fulfilling your obligations.

And busyness doesn't get you from where you are to where you want to go.

Below, there's a list of core values. Some will resonate with you more than others.

ACHIEVEMENT	HEALTH	POWER
AMBITION	HONESTY	PROFESSIONALISM
CARING	HUMOR	PUNCTUALITY
CHARITY	INDIVIDUALITY	QUALITY
COLLABORATION	INNOVATION	RECOGNITION
CREATIVITY	INTELLIGENCE	RELATIONSHIPS
CURIOSITY	INTUITION	RELIABILITY
DEPENDABILITY	JOY	RESILIENCE
EMPATHY	KINDNESS	RISK-TAKING
ENCOURAGEMENT	KNOWLEDGE	SAFETY
ENTHUSIASM	LEADERSHIP	SECURITY
ETHICS	LEARNING	SELF-CONTROL
EXCELLENCE	LOVE	SERVICE
FAIRNESS	LOYALTY	SPIRITUALITY
FAMILY	MAKING A DIFFERENCE	STABILITY
FRIENDSHIPS	MOTIVATION	SUCCESS
FLEXIBILITY	OPTIMISM	THANKFULNESS
FREEDOM	OPEN-MINDEDNESS	TRADITIONALISM
FUN	PASSION	UNDERSTANDING
GENEROSITY	PERFECTION	WEALTH
GROWTH	PERFORMANCE	WELL-BEING
HAPPINESS	PERSONAL DEVELOPMENT	WISDOM[5]
	POPULARITY	

---

5   Indeed editorial team, "6 Steps to Discover Your Core Values," June 2022, https://www.indeed.com/career-advice/career-development/discover-core-values.

At the end of this chapter, I invite you to return to your notes for your perfect day. In the *what* and *why* sections, ensure those activities and motivations align with your core values. Once they do, you'll wake up each morning excited, because you have a personal mission.

- With the core values on the previous page, write the five that resonate with you most. Number these in order of importance.

_____

_____

_____

_____

_____

_____

_____

_____

_____

_____

THE BUCKET METHOD

The key is not to prioritize what's on your schedule,
but to schedule your priorities.

—STEPHEN COVEY

It took time (years, in fact) for me to discover my *where*, *what*, and *why*—also my *who*. I've developed a system that schedules the ideal synergy between life fulfillment, personal growth, and professional success. I call it the bucket method, over which your core values act as an umbrella. I organize my time within these three buckets, ranked in order of importance. For me, this formula has stood the test of time.

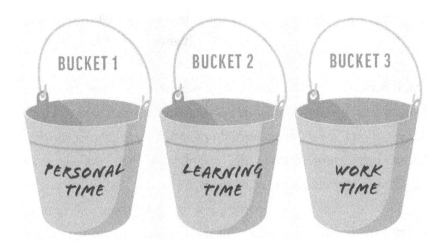

Bucket 1: Personal time. To lay this system out for you, my personal time is Anastasia. She and I sit down in the fall of each calendar year to look at the year ahead. We map out our January, February, March, April, May, June, and July through December. We find the vacation time. We find the long weekend time. We schedule random days off and holidays. We ask ourselves, Who do we want to spend that time with? Is it just us? Is it with friends? Is it with family? So bucket 1 is the priority.

Bucket 2: Learning. What do I want to learn in the coming year? Once I've hashed that out, I return to the calendar and plug it in, whether five days or ten days—however long that course or investment takes. Then I look at the rest of the year and discover my open windows to work. The only question I have to ask myself is, "Are there enough workdays to build enough revenue to pay for my bucket 1 and bucket 2?" When the answer is *yes*, I have bucket 3, and my calendar is complete. When the answer is *no*, I go back, reassess the year to come, and figure it out. Do I do a little less learning, or a little less personal time?

Realistically, I have to work enough days to pay for it all. And I also love what I do. The three buckets are a tool—a scheduling mechanism that prioritizes personal life first, learning life second, and then work life third. People still schedule their work lives first. The truth is that this doesn't lead to a higher level of fulfillment or success. After my colleague's tragedy and some introspection, I knew that if personal time and relationships weren't my priority, the success I already had was unsustainable. Personal time is about *who* you want to be with and *what* you want to do to enrich your life. An enriched human brings more to the table, regardless of their profession. An enriched human draws others to them.

Generationally, baby boomers live to work. They never learned to prioritize the personal time. But taking a page out of the millennial's book is a win. *Work to live.* It's a paradigm shift for the better. Boomers would perhaps agree that working to live is more valuable to them now than in their twenties or thirties. So maybe today, more than ever, our culture is finally shifting. But you have to design this life for yourself, first and foremost.

Segueing from the personal bucket, my second bucket helps me schedule time to get *better*, or else I'm just going to get trapped in that hamster wheel and wake up in two or five years not knowing any more than I knew then. Everyone who had invested time in learning while I did nothing will have passed me by.

To reiterate, the bucket that makes bucket 1 and bucket 2 possible is your professional career. Am I working enough days to fulfill my most essential buckets? Am I generating enough income to invest in my learning so I can get better? Am I working enough to support my personal life, and to live it the way that I want? If I'm not, I adjust my buckets, but if I don't begin with the end in mind—what kind of personal life I want to enjoy—I have no idea what learning I need to do or how much professional work I need to accomplish.

As you can see, these buckets interact and support one another, and the system is self-organizing. How much money do you need to support a rich life that has nothing to do with money? If you're making it up as you go along, you'll wonder why your life feels confused and off track. But when you structure your buckets early on, front ending what you want, you'll have a life designed for personal fulfillment.

This structure gets you from where you are to where you genuinely want to go.

It's easy to think in simplistic terms. You want that big house, that great car, and you think you want a boat or vacation, the whole nine yards. But what is the deeper meaning behind your wants? Is that vacation about family? Is the boat about adventure and spending time with friends? Is the big house about inviting more people into your life or creating more space for yourself?

Look for the deeper meaning, and patterns will emerge. Prioritize your personal life, prioritize your growth, work in a field that fills you with passion, but know that your ultimate success doesn't come from working to live.

- Now that you understand the bucket method, take note of your current buckets. Where is the majority of your time going? List three things.

_____

_____

_____

_____

_____

_____

_____

_____

STEEPING CORE VALUES INTO YOUR BUCKETS

Perhaps the most significant thing a person can know about himself is to understand his own system of values. Almost every thing we do is a reflection of our own personal value system. What do we mean by values? Our values are what we want out of life.

—JACQUES FRESCO

My professional career is propelled by my core values. I want to be the best at what I do. Work wouldn't fulfill me if I wasn't fully engaged in my career. Work would *exclusively* be a means to make money and fund my other goals in life. Instead of it being within my big picture, the professional bucket would be a box to check. By design, work is one of my buckets because it's a personal passion of mine—without letting it take over other priorities.

Working backward, what do I need to do to be the best at my job? I must follow Malcolm Gladwell's theory: "It takes 10,000 hours of intensive practice to achieve mastery of complex skills and materials." This perspective takes me to the learning bucket, where I discover the things I need to be better at tomorrow than I am today. The learning bucket is fundamental because, you know, life changes! Technology changes. People's wants and needs change. So whatever field you're in, if the learning bucket doesn't come before the professional bucket, you'll fall behind.

I can no longer use most of the skill sets I learned in dental school twenty-eight years ago, other than maybe the *philosophy* behind skill sets. But as for the actual utilization of everything I learned, none of it is the same. I hope you see how learning is more important than the time spent working. Education guarantees your continued success in work, and when it comes to what you like to do recreationally, learning feeds the soul.

Still, if I can teach you anything, it's that a quality-driven life isn't possible without bucket 1—your personal health, living situation, and relationships. As I've said, "Fake it till you make it" is a myth. You might be able to pull off a hot mess at home for a few weeks, but you can't pull it off long term. When you bring your best self to your professional life, while investing in *yourself*, money and success will come naturally.

After all, you know by now that your professional success shouldn't be driven by money. The profession you choose should be aligned with your core values. Your work is tied to your core values when you know your career makes you who you want to be. That's what makes it a part of your drive because there's a genuine desire to succeed—to learn more and improve in your field.

It brings up a larger discussion about money as a driving factor in your life. I think we've probably all met people who, on Friday or Saturday nights, were a bartender or a server—or maybe this was or *is* your lifestyle. You make a lot of money on the weekends. I remember going to these hot spots after a long week of dental school—much fun to be had.

Here's the thing: that guy who became accustomed to making a lot of money on Friday and Saturday nights is still there. It's easy for young people to get locked into a job where they make a lot of money, but it's hard for them to leave when they get accustomed to a lifestyle. They've already lost time when they figure out who they want to be. I suggest putting the money on hold and locking down what's in your personal, learning, and professional buckets.

If you want to get ahead in life and make a move, you'll have to take one or two steps back from the money you're making today.

You heard that right. Money that doesn't come from your passion isn't doing anything for you. Many get stuck in these income-driven jobs because they have already bought a big house and fancy car or are accustomed to the crazy vacations. It's too easy to get stuck when taking a significant step in life. Getting trapped is easy when taking a leap means a short-term pay cut. Think about this. It seems risky, but it's not. It's the ultimate investment in your future perfect day—your future perfect life. Your big picture.

From the start, we're all used to not having money. When I came out of school, I was used to living on terrible food in small spaces and having a ten-year-old car. That was just my life. That's the time to hold on for a little longer, gassing the pedal toward meaningful progress. If you choose money from day one, the odds of returning and redesigning your life diminish with time. But hey, it's still very much possible. Numbskull David Rice pivoting at forty-five is the perfect example, and although I want to guide those trying to figure all this out from an early start, I also want to advise you, no matter where you are on this journey.

I was an anomaly. I reached adulthood and thought, *You know what? I'm not doing this dentistry thing full-time anymore. I'm moving on. So I'll have to suck it up for a few years.* I still had a passion for dentistry, but I wanted to create Ignite. I wanted to teach. I craved the fusion between what I know as a dentist and my desire to inspire others. This shift didn't require heavy lifting or overtime. It required stepping back and realizing that getting where I wanted to go could require *less*. You know, I've never met anyone in the last days of their life who said, "Man, I wish I'd worked more. I wish I'd made more money."

You'll wish you would have surrounded yourself with loved ones—spent more time with your kids or friends or taken a trip.

Life's regrets are more significant than a paycheck. When it comes to your career, invest in the passion-infused marathon, not the sprint. Figure out who you want to be and build your essential team around you. It might take a bit longer. Maybe you'll be one of the lucky ones, and you fast-track. But if you're willing to put that time in on the front end, it will always pay you back tenfold, a hundredfold, a thousandfold, when you finally get to that other side—when you have an infrastructure for it.

Your buckets will help you build this solid infrastructure, and the groundwork you create will bolster you when life gets messy. Yep, it does get messy, but your core values are still your lighthouse.

CORE VALUES AND RELATIONSHIPS

Love is our most basic human value and also our highest potential.

—KAMAND KOJOURI

I'm blessed with a brilliant wife. My balance tends to get thrown off, and sometimes Anastasia will say to me, "David, remember what you said? You're out of balance. You made me promise to tell you that you were out of balance."

It's not all cut and dry. If you have your three buckets in order and are organizing your life accordingly, you're on the right track. But your core values are still your overhead sky, your underground earth, and not everyone's core values will align with yours. Your personal bucket is personal to *you*, your learning bucket is different from others, and your professional bucket is also unique. Your core values will be different from your spouse's, friends', and colleagues', which can lead to conflict. Going back to my cousin who ditched the beach and returned to work, his choices severely impacted his relationship. His wife had followed him all over the world for nearly thirty years, and when he retired, she perhaps thought, "This is finally our time."

A year and a half later, he'd changed his mind. Personal buckets had collided.

Discovering your core values early on will lead to a more meaningful and successful partnership with anyone. Finding your significant other's, your business partner's, and your inner circle of friends' core values is also key. Those who are meaningful to us are different from us. Still, if we openly communicate with them, we'll know how to navigate obstacles that might arise concerning another person's values when they don't align with our own.

It's common to wake up one day when you're thirty, forty, or fifty years old and say, "This relationship isn't what I thought it would be. This life isn't what I thought it would be." I would argue that it's because people don't define their priorities early on and don't live them out each day. Just as important, they don't understand the preferences of their partner or team. There are people in your life who add so much value that you won't kick them to the curb simply because core values don't align. At first, Anastasia and I didn't align, so we talked about it. We got past it through communication and understanding, as well as the willingness to sacrifice for the ultimate *who* you can ever imagine in your life. That's when you communicate to figure out how to make it work.

Life's an evolution. You're not supposed to stand in one place, but excellent communication is the way to traverse conflicting core values. My action is potentially somebody else's reaction, and then their reaction potentially becomes my reaction, and so on. When you're working with an entire team, that's a chain reaction of individuals with different motives and values.

When you don't hold firm to your core values—steeped in your buckets—any lane gets you off track in a hurry. (More about lanes in chapter 5.) And although balance is fundamental, in my experience, getting your personal bucket nailed down first is a must. It makes the other stuff more manageable. My cousin put his professional bucket first and had a lot to show for it. His life was impressive. But what meaning did it have with a personal bucket that had been neglected for years?

I hope you're beginning to grasp that the work of finding your *where*, *what*, and *why*, blocking your perfect day, defining your core values, and scheduling your buckets comes down to this: *Who* do you want to be? There's a good chance you have an answer to this question, but you might think it's impossible from where you stand. In the next chapter, I'll show you how it *is* possible.

TAKEAWAYS

- Core values are your beacons.
- Core values become your *why*, guiding you to your perfect day.
- Use the bucket method: personal, learning, and professional.
- Defining your core values early on will enhance your relationships and lead to better communication.
- For more guidance, go to drdavidrice.com/resources to read "Developing Your Values. " In the corresponding video, I discuss the process of defining core values.

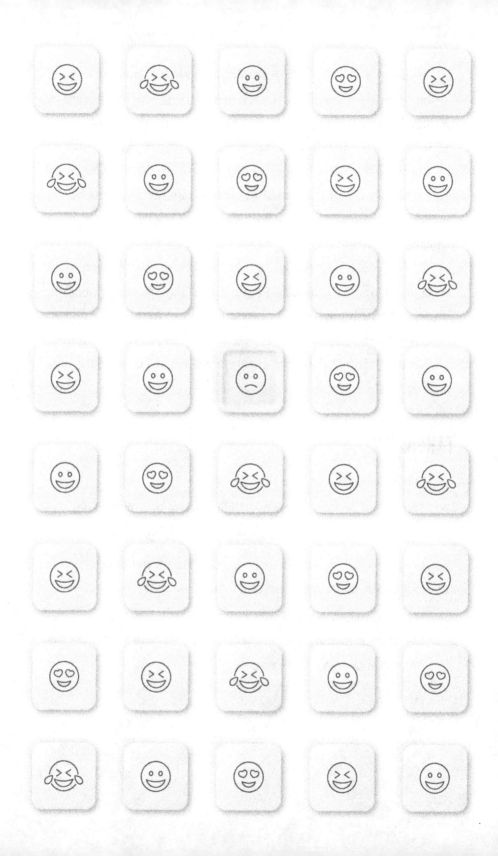

CHAPTER THREE

EVERYTHING IS POSSIBLE

The past, like the future, is indefinite and exists only as a spectrum of possibilities.

—STEPHEN HAWKING

A couple of years into owning my practice, I wanted to learn more. I wanted to *be* more. I was making the rounds at dental conferences, and the speakers were mesmerizing. One in particular was incredibly talented as a dentist, and as a speaker he was a rock star. That was it for me. That was the guy I wanted to be. I was petrified of speaking in front of large crowds, but I didn't want to let it beat me. I had a goal that seemed impossible from where I sat, but I was willing to take all the necessary steps.

When I first took a stab at it, I was terrified, and I remember sweating through my shirt. The nerves were overwhelming. I wondered if I was leading myself down a path that wasn't meant for me, but walking through the door of impossibility led to the greatest lesson of my life: you can learn how to do anything when you study and prepare. Everything is possible when you put in the effort and repeat, repeat, repeat.

It's funny how our brains trick us. They tell us where we are at is all we can manage. But once you have a vision, once you put in the effort, you wake up one day and what you initially envisioned is simply what you do. Today, people meet me and comment that what I do looks so effortless—creating videos or speaking at events. I have to laugh to myself because I want to say, "You should have met me a few years ago. It wasn't easy at all."

My career didn't end where it began. If I can impart anything to professionals of all ages, it's that your first career choice can be a launching pad to something more fulfilling. I was a successful dentist, but key mentors inspired me to want to achieve larger goals. I had to seek this inspiration out because I wasn't raised in an environment that already provided it for me.

I'll tell you this. Whatever you want to do in this life—I didn't have a dentist, entrepreneur, lawyer, etc. in the family—not being *raised* into your profession can't and won't stop you. The truth is that you're at an *advantage* when you need to start on your own. You're going to be better at what you do because of it. You might think having no initial guidance will hurt your chances. In reality, it's a gift. I never had anyone who framed my story. I had the opportunity to *discover* my story. There was no family pressure, and there was no one directing me. I made all my decisions. In reality, this couldn't have been done if my parents hadn't taught me that everything was possible and showed me the value of work.

And I did put in the work.

THE ANSWER TO HOW IS YES

If somebody offers you an amazing opportunity but you are not sure you can do it, say yes—then learn how to do it later!

—RICHARD BRANSON

You can learn to do anything, and when it comes to the scariest feats, you'll learn them better because you have that drive. But you can't do it alone! With any achievement, some people already have the experience and answers, and seeking out those people will fast-track your journey. Your *what* in life, your *why* in life—none of this is possible without *who* is in your life to help you.

In school, I was always the kid who couldn't stand the smartest person in the room. You know the type—they showed up to high school homeroom, borrowed my notebook for twenty minutes, and nailed the exam. Meanwhile, I spent hours learning this stuff and still struggled.

I was diligent but didn't always excel in school. This helped me to realize a couple of things. One, we all have different learning styles, and part of gaining intelligence is *learning how you learn best*. Understand that your handicaps can become your strengths. And two, the *workers* always outdo the traditionally smart people. "Hard work beats talent when talent doesn't work hard," says Tim Notke.

It doesn't matter how smart you are. If the work ethic isn't built in, aptitude won't take you anywhere. If you don't take the time to foster this infrastructure for yourself, your talent has nothing to carry it or make it grow. When you're willing to work, you realize you don't have to be great tomorrow. You just need to be *better* tomorrow and keep that up every single day.

Discovering your core values, infusing these into your perfect day—these habits take you from the impossible to the possible. Because I promise you that everything is possible.

Over the years, I've become friends with a dental rep named Dan. He comes in and sells things that are useful for our profession. Most dentists view their rep as a pain in their backsides because he's a person who is just trying to sell them something. Now, I've always thought that you can learn something from everyone, so when I first met Dan, I was super young and said to him, "I have a question for you. What's the difference between the people who are really happy and successful as dentists and everyone who is not?"

He smiled and replied, "They say *yes*."

This reminded me of an important Peter Block quote: "The answer to how is yes."

Say *yes* to hard work. Say *yes* to possibilities, even when you don't know how to turn them into a reality. God knows, I'm not asking you to be a people pleaser or a "yes man/woman." Don't do the grunt work simply because your boss is telling you to. Take the initiative to say *yes* to the hard work that will drive you toward your big picture—your vision. This work is often scary, and you might not know where it will take you.

It's taking you somewhere you thought you could only dream of.

- In the space below, write three things you can say yes to. These bring you closer to the goals that seem impossible. Is there a specific course? A networking opportunity? Perhaps there are some books you can order to expand your horizons.

_____

_____

_____

_____

CHASE THE DREAM—EVEN WHEN THE OUTCOME ISN'T CLEAR

All I'm saying is that to liberate the potential of your mind, body and soul, you must first expand your imagination. You see, things are always created twice: first in the workshop of the mind and then, and only then, in reality.

—ROBIN SHARMA, *THE MONK WHO SOLD HIS FERRARI*

We all have the same twenty-four hours in a day. Most of my friends are usually too busy—they have kids or they have this and that. I've never verbalized this to them, but I call it BS. What you do with your twenty-four hours is your choice. So you can choose, first of all, to tell yourself you don't have the time—you can choose to waste two hours a day watching television and anything else for that matter—*or* you can also choose to use your time to build the life you want. When it's a priority, that's where you direct your time.

"Patience is a virtue." Kind of.

Being patient with people you love is a virtue, but being patient for your career and success is garbage. You have to go and get it! You have to make it happen because no one is going to hand it to you.

After seeing those dental professionals at the front of the room during conferences, something clicked inside me. I wanted to be an influential dentist. I wanted to be respected, published, and a leader in my field. I also wanted a legacy that left my profession better than when I found it. My career goals, my lane, turned into a fusion of what I loved—dentistry and teaching. Connecting with people and growing together. It was my impossible.

I would ask those I looked up to, "What do I need to do? What specifically do others want?" The answer was profound: it wasn't about what anyone else wanted; it was about what *I* wanted. If you want to be an influential dentist, you should document everything. Then one day, you'll be able to sit back and see what you've accomplished—what worked and what didn't work. Make the decision that you have a dream and then chase that dream. It won't happen on its own.

When your dream is important enough, excuses won't get in the way. You just keep building, because you already see the end result and have the conviction to push through barriers. You may not recognize what the most important pieces are, but you just keep doing it because eventually you'll have the clarity. Your efforts will provide you with a bank of information—maybe from books you've read, things you've studied, or people you've met and followed. You'll have all this access to things no one else has spent any time on.

> WHEN YOUR DREAM IS IMPORTANT ENOUGH, EXCUSES WON'T GET IN THE WAY.

Speaking of documenting your life's work, I got a call from a retired friend in the dental field. As it turns out, for forty years he'd documented everything he did on every patient. He had close to two hundred thousand images. All that work for forty years, and he had no idea what to do with it all. One day, a patient of his, who happened to be a media person, listened to my friend mention, "I'm going to retire, and I have all this stuff. I'm just going to trash it!"

The patient was in awe. "What are you talking about? You have a lifetime of information. Can you imagine what you could teach somebody who is one year out, five years out, ten years, or twenty?"

The dentist had a change of heart after this and asked for my advice. I told him how impressive his documentation was and advised that he collate the photos so we could categorize them. I reiterated that we could teach a lot of people countless things from his diligent work. As it turned out, he'd already collated the photos every year—organized in lanes. The collection was all set.

He put in the work.

Why was I shocked by this? Because here was this guy, seventy years old, who wanted to retire but still be helpful and relevant. He wanted to contribute to his field. His years of effort left him with something almost nobody I know has, because he put in the work, even when he didn't know where it would take him. For forty years, he put in consistent effort, which left him with a very important contribution.

Even when the dream isn't clear, keep doing the work. It will take you somewhere, even if it's just an important legacy. Document it because it's all *meaningful for others*.

Your legacy isn't just about being impressive in your field. It comes down to helping people, and that retired dentist will continue to influence many with what he's achieved. More about this kind of influence in part III, Your Personal Worth. This is big picture work.

DON'T SPRINT TO YOUR IMPOSSIBLE

Every weakness contains within itself a strength.

—SHŪSAKU ENDŌ, AUTHOR

We've already established that everyone will go at a different pace when creating the life they want. Everyone learns and processes things differently. I would advise that you avoid the sprint unless it's happening naturally for you.

The problem is, in the digital age, we're allowed access to everyone's lives 24-7—people putting their best foot forward to be seen in the optimal light. When you're not where you want to be, the tendency is to sprint. You want instant results because you already feel behind. Don't let the perfect posts on social media fool you. Individuals jump into things and make hasty decisions that they think will power them forward. The reality is that most end up running in unfocused circles or, even worse, in the wrong direction.

Take a breath. Success won't happen overnight.

Listen, it *does* happen. When you see an overnight success, I guarantee that you don't know the whole story. It comes one of three ways. Some get there as legacy success stories. They come from the mom and dad who had $50 million in the bank. Others are in the exact right place at the right time. Let's be honest, there are great luck stories. The third and most common is the ten-year "overnight" success. They put in the work. Malcolm Gladwell's *The Tipping Point*[6] goes into this phenomenon in detail. For any one of these three examples, maybe the winner went to a great school and had a mentor who was a 2 percenter. Never underestimate the power of that. I'll use the term "2 percenter" a lot in this book—a term coined by Brendon Burchard referring to the top echelon of any field.

Think about it. If you knew at age fifteen that you wanted to be a dentist, just happened to find the most skilled dentist in your state, and apprenticed them—holy cow—imagine all the lessons you'd learn from the start! With the right work ethic, you'd be set. Not only would you learn more than you ever could in school, but you'd also gain fundamental life lessons from that mentor. There are countless reasons for why some people get a really strong head start, but most of us inch along in life. The good news is that inching along makes you stronger in the end.

It's important to get comfortable with slow forward progress, so long as you're making *consistent* progress. If you hit stopping points,

---

6   Malcolm Gladwell, *The Tipping Point: How Little Things Can Make a Big Difference* (Boston: Little, Brown and Company, 2000).

if you're stuck and don't know how to get out, that's when you need your cheerleader, contrarian, and 2 percenter. We'll discuss these key mentors in chapter 8.

When you sprint, you tune people out and lean into what you know. When you grasp the big picture, you rely on the knowledge of others and lean into *what you don't know*.

Don't strengthen what is working for you. Do a deep dive into what's challenging and not working. Take the time to do it right, and the earlier the better. There's no need to compare yourself to others. Their vision isn't yours, and their upbringing isn't yours. You have unique challenges and also unique possibilities. Put in the work and find your *who*—your team, your mentors, and your inspirations. Know that it's possible and keep plugging away every day.

Someone once presented me with the idea of living life backward. Basically, instead of trying to get to this special place where you can finally become the person you want to be—so you can finally *do* the things you want to do in life—be that person today. Do those things, and that's what will help you become the person you want to become. Hard work, mentors, and education will take you there. You can't fail if you don't quit—at anything!

As you know from bucket 2, *becoming* comes from consistent self-education—education regarding yourself, the world, and your field. Life changes so quickly, and the simplest analogy is technology. We all see how technology changes, but what we fail to understand is how quickly whatever business you're in, whatever profession you're in, whatever walk of life you're in, also changes. If you don't constantly learn, it won't be more than a year before you're behind. Never stop. Keep going.

You're the most productive in the first five years of your career, because you have all this energy. Young people have the energy, and old people have the wisdom, and then there's this sweet spot where you combine that energy with the wisdom. The more wisdom you can gain quickly along the way, while you still have the *energy*, the further you'll go.

If you're in the right lane for the right reasons because it's a core value for you, you won't get tired too quickly. So the faster you learn, the more you capitalize on that energy. The more you're in love with what you do, the longer that energy stays, which buys you time to keep learning. The bucket method will continuously propel you forward.

But don't just learn what you already know. Don't learn what comes easy to you. That is the area where you need the least education. Focus on what comes the hardest. No one wants to do this, but your weak spots do become your strengths.

Adults who go back to college are often better students than the youth who surround them. The reason? They *want* to be there. They've discovered this core value for themselves. Not sprinting to your impossible means that you can start over again at your pace. This isn't a competition. Beginning fresh comes from a new kind of devotion and understanding of yourself. You'll learn what you need to learn because you're *all in*.

Schedule, schedule, schedule learning time. It doesn't have to be twenty hours a day. Just find the time and plug it in. If you must go to night school instead of going all day, do that. If you like to work out and don't like to read, then get an audiobook and listen while you're walking, driving, running, cycling, or whatever you enjoy.

There are so many opportunities to learn while making the impossible possible.

FREE UP YOUR FUTURE BY UNDERSTANDING YOUR PAST

How many souls have failed to soar because they
were suffocated in a loved one's worry?

—BRENDON BURCHARD, *THE MOTIVATION MANIFESTO*

In my youth, I didn't have a concept of what was possible. My family was loving and supportive, but I didn't have a guide. My parents were very much lower middle class. Dad worked three jobs. Mom didn't go past high school because she felt like her family needed her to contribute, but Dad did go on to get his master's in education and became a teacher. Interestingly enough though, he didn't understand networking and was repulsed by it. For him, it was just kissing ass. He didn't want to be one of those people.

I don't blame him, but for me, as I went on in life, the *who* was the answer to going places.

My family had this crazy ceiling where money was evil and upward mobility was suspect. This is common, but what I learned in full force—and didn't understand at the time—was the power of work ethic. My dad's real job was teaching in Buffalo's public high schools. His other jobs consisted of working for a neighbor, plowing snow from one in the morning until the average dad was waking up for the day, and then, after teaching all day, he worked security at a wealthy person's mansion. My mother—talk about core values—gave up her banking career when my sister and I were born. As soon as we were both in school, she took a part-time job at our school. That way she could be home when we were home and work when we were out. While growing up, I witnessed my parents working what seemed like twenty-four-hour days. They did it for us. They never spoke about it. That was just what life was like so that we could go to private school.

Mom and Dad showed me what true work ethic looks like.

Despite all this, they still had time for me and my sister. Everything my parents did was for us. *Everything.* As you can see, this was when I got my understanding of hard work and also an understanding of when the balance is off.

I remember telling my parents, "I want to live in California or Florida. I want to be by the ocean where it's sunny all the time."

My mom lovingly responded, "David, if it's beautiful every day, at some point you just won't appreciate it anymore." That was her rationalization for staying in Buffalo. That was her rationalization for keeping her son around.

Our parents want to hold us close and feed us all the time. They mean what they say. They mean well. However, they don't necessarily grasp the psychological impact it has on us. The "sunshine will get boring" story told in our house became *my* story. When I met people who lived in a very nice place, my thoughts suggested, *If I had all the time in the world there, maybe I wouldn't appreciate it.* I'd internalized not going to my *where.*

Once I had my *aha* moment and moved to Florida, I thought, *I wake up every day and love it!* I look out of our windows in Tampa Bay and think there's no place I'd rather be than right here. It's a great feeling.

This isn't a travel endorsement for Florida—although I'm enthusiastic about it—but an endorsement for your big picture. What's holding you back in your head? Take stock in the fact that what's creating your impossible might be your upbringing. While growing up, I was aware of, "Children ought to be seen and not heard." My parents learned this colloquialism from someone else. I don't think parents realize that phrases like this can have a long-term effect. There are so many who walk into a room and wonder how they can get out of that room without anyone noticing. That was me.

I woke up one day and realized that avoiding social situations is not how you navigate life if you want to be successful—to succeed you need to make meaningful connections. Keeping your head down and not letting anyone notice you won't get you anywhere other than working for someone else your whole life. So for my parents, "Children ought to be seen and not heard" was innocent. But for the receiver? I think not. This notion led to me being a people pleaser my whole life, till I was on the verge of exploding. I didn't want to say *yes* one more time to anything other than my vision. All my *yeses* were pointed toward my big picture—not what others wanted from me but what I wanted for myself.

> I WOKE UP ONE DAY AND REALIZED THAT AVOIDING SOCIAL SITUATIONS IS NOT HOW YOU NAVIGATE LIFE IF YOU WANT TO BE SUCCESSFUL—TO SUCCEED YOU NEED TO MAKE MEANINGFUL CONNECTIONS.

We're all so unique, but we have our baggage and hiccups along the way. *Everything is possible* when you see that you're not like other people, and your big picture can't and shouldn't be denied. There are hurdles within yourself, and you have past experiences, but there's also the drama you come up against. All of this is meaningless.

Let's talk about drama next.

- Write five statements or actions from your past that gave you a limiting view of your future.

_____

_____

_____

_____

_____

TAKEAWAYS

- Everything is possible when you put in the effort and repeat, repeat, repeat.
- The answer to how is yes.
- Chase the dream without knowing the end result.
- Take your time reaching your impossible, as long as you're putting in the work.
- Understand your past. Don't let your upbringing limit your possibilities.
- Follow the "Tips for Developing a Vision for Your Future " at drdavidrice.com/resources and check out the next video via this link or the QR code.

CHAPTER FOUR

DITCH THE DRAMA— OVERCOME OBSTACLES

All war is a symptom of man's failure as a thinking animal.

—JOHN STEINBECK

Years ago, I met a great guy who happened to be the smallest Texan I'd ever seen—five foot five, which is not the scenario you'd picture. His name was Walter. Now, Walter was a very intelligent businessman who jumped into dentistry consulting because he knew dentists, in general, were terrible communicators.

He had great lessons to impart. I remember him looking at me and saying, "David, here's the deal. Anyone who brings negativity into your life [drama], you have to eliminate from your life. I don't care if it's your mother, father, child, or your best friend." He went on to say, "Send them a Christmas card, send them a ham—I don't care—but they cannot be a part of your day-to-day."

Walter's message stuck with me. You might have noticed by now that I tend to look at the world in black and white, rather than the gray in between. When it comes to handling negativity and drama, this is a good thing. I took his words to heart and asked myself, "Who in my life is helping me get to where I want to go, and who is not?"

Even if the *nots* weren't totally negative, if they weren't driving all the good stuff in my big picture, I decreased the frequency of time I spent with them. I decreased involvement because these weren't the people propelling my vision not only for my career but also for my well-being.

For the people in my life who were *fully* negative forces, they had to go. I needed to sit down with one of my best friends and say, "Hey, you're a great guy. We've known each other for a long time. We've gotten each other through some difficult times, but this is done. I can't …"

To delve deeper, this was a period in my life when I was pissed, angry, and way too cocky for my own good. I remember showing up to teach at the dental school on a Friday and thought, *Nobody knows I was out till four in the morning. I'm so good at what I do that they won't be able to tell.* It *might* have been crystal clear to everyone. I recall going so far as to say to a colleague that on my worst day I was twenty times better than everyone else in the building. That colleague should have thrown me out.

This kind of behavior stemmed from the fact that my best friend and I would have a little too much fun on Thursday nights with our companion, Jack Daniels. That's why I had to sit down with my friend and make a change. Neither of us were bad people, but I noticed the negative pattern and wanted to put an end to it. I couldn't break the cycle and still be buddies with him. It wouldn't work.

To this day, almost a decade later, I still send him messages on his birthday and Christmas, and vice versa. I ask him how he's doing, how the family's doing, and that's it. You can imagine how hard that initial conversation was. It's important to realize that you'll need to have some hard conversations with people when something isn't working—

when you need to ditch the drama. It's about setting boundaries and creating space for the people who are the best fit for you in life.

It's tricky business, so how do you know who is bringing drama and negativity? Your stomach creeps up. Your gut knows, and you must act upon this. You have no time to waste. There are signs that people aren't contributing. There are real symptoms. Follow your gut, stick to your vision, and hold yourself accountable. Only keep the people in your life who are supporting and fostering your vision.

To clarify, drama is conflict with no solution. Later in this chapter, we'll discuss the kinds of conflict there are solutions for, but first, let's examine drama.

UNPLUG THE DRAMA

Drama: A state, situation, or series of events involving interesting or intense conflict of forces.

—MERRIAM-WEBSTER

Yeah, it's interesting and intense. But I disagree. It's just noise.

We're hardwired for drama—dramatic people, shocking news, and events on social media. We're addicted to it. Sometimes, I have a bad feeling about a person or situation, so I approach my mentors and say, "I need you to tell me what you think. Steer me in the right direction. You know my vision for myself, and I need you to be honest about whether I'm closer or further away from stuff that doesn't support that vision."

Ditching drama in your personal life is one of the most difficult and rewarding steps you can take. We all love who we want to love. We all want to stay friends with the people we're friends with. We want to believe we can fix people in life, but in the end, we're each the only person who can fix our own lives. When something is not working in a relationship dynamic, you can't fix that person. All you can do is work on yourself.

I never read the news, ever. Walter gave me this guidance as well. I remember asking him, "Walter, really? Well, how do you stay informed?"

He replied, "Don't you believe if something really important is happening in the world, somebody around will tell you?"

And he's right. With the craziness happening in the world, people will keep me up to speed, but I refuse to get sucked into the negativity of the news. Not that those issues aren't important, but it's easy to wallow in them—it's easy to read one article and then read ten. It's easy to watch one channel and then want to watch more—being addicted to social media and going down the rabbit hole each day. Dose and limit the content, because you don't need twenty-four hours of complaining or people showing you how wonderful their lives are. It just makes you feel bad. Instead, use that focus to invest in your wonderful life. It's hardly ever a real win when you're on social media for more than twenty minutes, let alone two to three hours.

The best replacement? Surround yourself with the right people and activities that feed your brain. Whatever works for you.

Googling something, YouTubing something, or being on any form of social media—even reading and watching the news—is sucking the life out of you. Walter gets a lot of credit for the structure that I've created in my life. Again, this wasn't my strength at first, and it took time to create new habits, but I knew he was right and put in the work. I highly recommend you watch *The Social Dilemma* if you haven't already. It will change your life.

Drama is stimulating. You watch someone on TV get angry, and *you* get angry. You watch someone grieve, and *you* grieve. We're led to believe this is good for us—we're human. But when you unplug the drama and noise—the people who bring nothing but negativity—what will replace these?

Your life.

If you want that balance between your professional time and personal time, and in your personal time you're plugging in the right people, ditching the drama, and freeing up blocks, there will be some space to fill. That's now golden time—a golden block or two. That's the time to decompress in a way that turns you into who you want to be.

If you want to eat healthier, don't keep junk food in the house. That's a good start. But if you don't have healthy food to replace it, you'll get hungry and use Uber Eats to deliver the junk food. Why? You have to figure out some way to feed yourself. I look at feeding the brain in the same way. Ditch the drama and junk and replace them with true nourishment.

A book, the arts, spending time with someone you cherish, or allowing space for introspection are great places to start. Drama is an addiction that prevents you from spending time with real people or filling your blocks with activities that make you grow. It's also an addiction that takes away your power.

Many get caught in a loop and don't know how to just be happy! I mean, think about all the people you know. And I'm sure this has been me at some point in my lifetime. I was such a self-sabotaging person. In the back of my mind, when something was getting good, I had the inclination to kill it. I assumed that if I *didn't* kill it, someone would do it for me, and I preferred to bypass the future hurt. This is the kind of drama that we internalize. When we spend too much time watching others' lives—lives filled with negativity—we lose sight of everything being possible.

There is so much out there to learn from. There are great books to read or listen to, documentaries to watch. Figure out what works for you and *learn, learn, learn.* Study great people—surround yourself with great people!—read quotes or get into history. You'll find that you start to notice patterns and see the world differently. You grow from researching others' successes.

> SUCCESS IN ANY OTHER LANE WILL BRING YOU SUCCESS IN YOUR LANE.

Success in any other lane will bring you success in your lane. Approach the successes of others with undying curiosity. Take your time to learn about human potential. Yes, even failure. Ditching the drama seems like swimming upstream, but it also opens up time to feed your mind.

- Calculate the amount of time you spend on social media each day. Now, list three activities you could be doing in that time that move you closer to your big picture.

_____

_____

_____

PREPARE YOURSELF TO BE THE CALM IN THE STORM

The price of greatness is responsibility over each of your thoughts.

—WINSTON CHURCHILL

The calm in the storm provides solutions, not problems.

I recall an emergency I'd encountered years back. I was at a holiday party, and at one point a gentleman just dropped down to the ground. Boom. There were maybe thirty people there. So when something like this happens, ask yourself, "Who do I want to be?" Do you want to be the person panicking in the corner? Do you want to be the one trying to escape? Or do you want to be the individual everyone in the room looks to because they know you'll make it better?

In that moment of crisis, my first instinct was to look for the ER doctor in attendance, but, of course, he'd just walked out to work his shift.

That left me.

Yeah, I'm just a dentist, but I at least knew CPR and the whole nine yards. I approached, got down, and assessed if the guy was okay. I noticed that he was breathing, and he had a pulse, so I wasn't sure why he passed out. That was something to figure out. My brain clicked into work mode. We needed to call 911. To make matters more complicated, this was a rooftop party. I started to give orders: "*You* need to get to the elevator and hold it," and "*You* need to get to the other elevator, go downstairs, and hold it when the EMTs get here," and "And then *you*. I appreciate you. You're trying to help, but you're telling this guy to take a deep breath and hold it because you practice yoga and meditation. That's not the right advice. That's not what we do. So thank you very much. You're amazing. But we won't be doing that."

I didn't say that last quote out loud, but you get the gist.

The point is that the guy ended up being okay. People trusted my orders because I was calm at that moment—problem-solving. I'd spent countless hours practicing being calm in heightened situations. So in the workplace, how do you habituate being calm during unexpected events? It takes training—both in life and in your career. I had a game plan because I'd been taking BLS—basic life support— and ACLS—advanced cardiac life support—since I was twenty-six years old.

I was the person everyone in the room looked to because I'd trained to be calm. I had a certain temperament and a temporary solution.

I'm a big *Seinfeld* fan, and there's this episode where George Costanza is at a kids' birthday party. At the time, his girlfriend was one of the teachers. There's smoke in the kitchen, and he's the panicked one. George pushes children and teachers out of the way to escape the building. The scene is hilarious, and the reason it's so funny is because George is the shining example of who you *don't want to be*. You'd never look at that person the same way again.

How you collect yourself is a measure of not only your character but also your training. *Handling* intensity takes training! A focused effort to be the calm in the storm will help you collect yourself in any given situation. How do you get into a good headspace so that you're coming from a solution-oriented place? The key to handling conflict is this: I'm not trying to be right. I'm trying to solve something with you.

If you're the kind of person who figures things out with others, people will be attracted to you. By all means, if you're in an emergency and you have the most knowledge in the room, calmly instruct others on how they can help. The bigger point is that you are the calm in the storm when you (a) are trained to be calm and (b) work with others.

This is a process. In the professional world, examine the last ten times something blew up. Were you the calmest in the room, or was it someone else? If it was someone else, you'll look to them in the future, and that person has a huge win. The calmest person in the room triumphs because they're the leader.

In the workplace, you know what you'll be faced with 80 percent of the time—20 percent of the time will be a surprise. If you train yourself *well* for the 80 percent, you can handle the 20 percent. Being well versed in the 80 percent makes you the calm in the storm.

In any career endeavor, ask yourself, "Okay, what are all the things that could go wrong? What *happens* when they go wrong? Who do I want to be when it goes wrong *here, here*, and *here*?"

Again, this doesn't happen overnight. You prepare yourself for these events. There were plenty of times when I wasn't the calm person in the storm and I needed somebody to dial me down. Eventually, I learned to reflect and see that I could have done better. I asked for critique. The conversation might look like this: "Hey, that didn't go well. How did I do? Could I have done better? Give me a grade from one to ten. Okay, I'm an eight. How do I get to a ten?"

Let people—especially your mentors—tell you what you can improve to be the calm in the storm—the one who others look to.

These lessons are for everyone, but understand that vulnerability levels you up as a leader—*positions* you to leadership. Almost no one thinks to ask the above questions—not just asking your mentors but also asking your team. When your team sees you asking questions, they think, *He doesn't have all the answers but actually wants to know what I need when the sh*t hits the fan.*

Being willing to learn from those around you is a character trait showing low drama and incredible intention. And if you can learn from the others, that communication is also part of the preparation— here are the events, here's the worst it can get, how I want to respond, here are the people I work with, and here's what they need from me when that happens, etc.

Prepare yourself to be the calm in the storm—certainly as the leader—but no matter what your position, this will elevate your worth. There's more to come on this in chapter 10.

- List five situations in which you foresee conflict might arise. Beside each, write one solution to be the calm in the storm.

_____

_____

_____

_____

_____

OVERCOME OBSTACLES BY FINDING SOLUTIONS

This is the tyranny of impoverished thinking. Those people who think the same thoughts every day, most of them negative, have fallen into bad mental habits. Rather than focusing on all the good in their lives and thinking of ways to make things even better, they are captives of their pasts.

—ROBIN SHARMA

Both drama and conflict come from power struggles. There are power-hungry people in this world who crave these. Some are struggling to find power in the moment because they feel very much out of control, or they felt powerless for most of their lives. Power-hungry people seek conflict because they want control. I know many who love conflict—they eat it up and like the debate. They want to prove how smart they are or prove how much money they have.

They want to prove *anything*.

Most of this behavior is rooted in insecurity. Every bully out there is cruel because they're hiding something, and that's their way—that's their mask. Some people curl up, and other people fight, which is human. Fight or flight. But there's another option. There's the person who stands inside the conflict and looks to *resolve* it.

Another win when being the calm in the storm is that when you're grounded, prepared for a difficult situation, you think clearly—more than anyone else who is interacting in the situation. I've never claimed to be the smartest guy in the room, but I see that when you stay calm and someone else is hot—when they're intentionally trying to fuel something—you can diffuse the situation. *That is authentic power.*

Others around you will notice this grounded approach. They'll naturally think the other guy is a jerk. When you are the leveled voice in the room, others recognize the dramatic voices, and they'll know who to look to in the future. So reacting calmly and intentionally—I don't want to say *strategically* because that's loaded—is the *response* to any situation that will take everyone where they want to go. They're looking up to someone focused on resolution.

The calm person in the room is the one in control.

Conflict happens, but there's just no room for indulging in it when you know your *where, what,* and *why*—when you have your core values lined up and the big picture focus is clear. Internalizing this approach makes drama a waste of your time and conflict something to be resolved. And if something *can't* be resolved, it's a waste of your time.

To put it bluntly, you have better things to do.

When you're on your path, you don't need to prove that you're smarter, faster, stronger, or better—that you're right. After you've taken the time to define your big picture, you root for *others*! Their accomplishments don't intimidate you. They inspire you.

I'll end this chapter by shifting gears to the most important relationships in your life and how these principles can apply to them—specifically, conflict in your bucket 1. In these situations, it's equally important to be the calm in the storm. This one is tricky. You might have discovered that amid personal conflict, others want an immediate response. They want you to have the answers. I just don't believe this is true. It's okay to pause and take a breath. Let's say Anastasia and I are having a conversation, and something isn't going well. This is my wife. She's not trying to make me mad or make life worse. She's working to get us to a better place and share something important that she hasn't been able to share before.

Good communication requires introspection. In many situations, I find myself thinking, *Oh man, that didn't come out exactly the way I wanted it to.* As humans, we often are afraid we misspoke. In any personal conflict, it's important to step back and ask yourself what's really being said. What's actually happening here? When in doubt, active listening is key, as well as *communicating* what you think you're hearing. For instance, "What I'm hearing is this. Am I hearing right?"

More often than you think, you're hearing wrong. That's not what the other person was saying at all. Without taking the time to get it right, miscommunication leads to drama and conflict. You see, your job isn't to be right. Your job is to figure out how to get past whatever the conflict is with those you truly want in your life. When it comes to Anastasia, I don't need to be right. We love each other. We care about one another. There's no contest. This is a bucket that's worth the time and effort.

I often stop and ponder how much smoother life, happiness, and success would be once I learn to treat all my relationships like I've learned to treat Anastasia. I feel like this is the ultimate place to get to. We all have that one person in our lives who is the barometer. If we can have the patience to treat others like we treat our bucket 1 individual—the source of our true love and devotion—then we finally learn how to treat all people.

I come back to the 80/20 percent rule. Something is always going to hit the fan. A psychologist friend told me years ago, "You know *you*, so when you're hot and know it won't go anywhere, then have the ability in those couple of seconds to regroup. Instead of thinking of what to say, realize that the interaction is important." It's okay to inform someone that you want to talk, but you're feeling a little too hot at the moment. It's okay to ask for ten minutes or even a day. Go for a walk. Destress in whatever way you need. With someone you care about, it's valid to admit that the discussion is important—it will happen—but you'd rather take the time to come from a good place.

- In the end, it's simple. Letting go of drama and negativity, as well as finding resolutions to conflict, comes from knowing yourself enough to stop wasting time on what's not serving you.

TAKEAWAYS

- Unplug negative people and drama.

- Be the calm in the storm and *prepare* yourself to be that person.

- Conflict management isn't about being right. It's about solving problems.

- Authentic power comes from asking questions and listening.

- You've got better things to do than linger on drama or conflict.

- Check out my next blog, "Tips for Removing Negative People from Your Life." As always, enjoy the complementary video at drdavidrice.com/resources or by using the QR code.

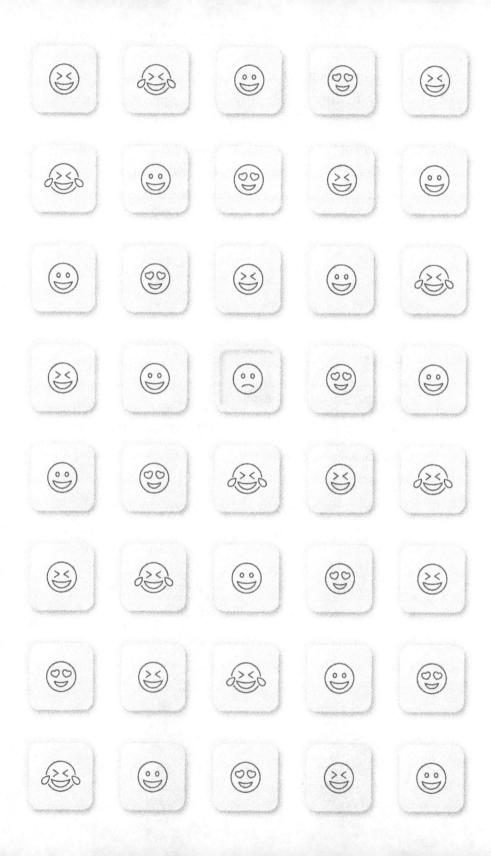

CHAPTER FIVE

FINDING YOUR LANE

*Most people dabble their way through life,
never deciding to master anything in particular.*

—TONY ROBBINS

I had a meeting with someone I was interested in bringing onto our Ignite team—a freelancer. She offered to build out some content for us, did her research, and then consulted her advisors who suggested a fee.

Her response was, "It will cost you $5,000 per hour for the job."

I laughed, saying, "Listen, I'm going to unplug my business hat and plug in my friend hat. You're so out of the ballpark with your number. I've lost all interest in carrying this conversation forward. You'll never get that dollar amount."

I was being honest with her and received radio silence until she asked, "Well, can we negotiate?"

I had to tell her that this wasn't a negotiation—this was a professional arrangement. But someone told her to do it that way, and she just shot herself in the foot with me and anyone who asks if I'd recommend her.

Harsh? No, this is reality. People tend to hire others when they sense the applicant is operating entirely in their lane.

How did I know this person wasn't in their lane? Why did I not wish to support her professional career? She was more interested in fast money than building a relationship and delivering real value. Finding and defining your lane brings out your character. You prove you're in your lane when you take it slow, build over time, and recognize the value of those you network with. Your lane defines you—it's your niche—and when you're truly on your path, your values show through.

The problem is people often jump at *every* opportunity because they're afraid that the moment will get away—they get distracted by all the opportunities there are in the world. (More on the "fear of missing out" to come.) The good news is that when you define your lane, and also realize you can build a brand for yourself, then people will flock to you because you're *exceptional* at something. And your heart is in it.

> IF YOU DON'T DEFINE WHAT YOU'RE KNOWN FOR, THE WORLD WILL DEFINE IT FOR YOU.

That professional shot herself in the foot because she wasn't long-gaming her approach. She was sprinting because her vision wasn't there, her core values weren't aligned, and she was money grabbing. Ultimately, defining your lane is a call to action because if you don't define what you're known for, the world will define it for you.

Don't be a jack-of-all-trades. I would argue that your niche wins 1,000 percent of the time. There's incredible power in defining and staying true to your path—your calling, your passion, and your end goal. This process takes time. As we discussed in chapter 3—don't sprint—your lane requires dedication.

Stay focused. Spend 80 percent of your time in your lane and 20 percent on stuff that puts food on the table. Most succumb to putting 20 percent of their time into their lane and 80 percent on expenses. But when you sacrifice, put in the research, put in the work, and stay focused, your lane *will* feed you. You'll eventually be living your vision—your impossible.

I ask you this: What's the one thing you want to be known for? Practice that skill as often as you can and with integrity. Slow down. Be humble. Your lane can be clearly defined but getting to it is also a process—a process of broadening and then funneling. I'll explain.

BROADEN YOUR HORIZONS

Each destination you reach only opens out into wider horizons,
new and undiscovered countries for you to explore.

—BARBARA SHER

Your lane is a narrow and focused path—it's your niche. But before you define it, go broad.

Exposing yourself to as many possibilities as you can, as soon as you can, is a win. We've talked about the curse of social media. You can ditch the drama and the rabbit hole aspect of it, but there's a golden vein in social media that we *haven't* discussed. The great blessing comes from constructively *exploring* through social media. You can go on an adventure without having the money to travel. You can learn about a 2 percenter in your industry. You can connect with people who encourage you—join forums that interest you. These are *constructive* uses of social media.

Let's discuss how to use social media correctly via podcasts, virtual and in-person meetups, as well as reading or listening to materials that move you ahead in life—instead of taking up your time and mental health. Basmo is a reading app whose statistics show that "88 percent of rich people devote thirty minutes or more each day to self-education or self-improvement reading," and "Bill Gates says that reading is 'the main way that I both learn new things and test my understanding.' His love for reading is what has exposed the tech mogul to a world of opportunities."[7]

There's a correlation between the frequency with which people read books and the success they achieve. Reading is the easiest and simplest way to expose us to so many things—broadening our horizons. *Listen* (see what I did there?), some people don't like to read. I digest most of my books through sound. I know my learning style. Audio books count too! You can listen in the car or on the treadmill.

Read, listen, and watch as much as you can. If that's through social media, so be it. As long as it's feeding you and not depleting you.

Google is a powerful tool for wasting time, but it's also a powerful tool for finding mentors. Always ask yourself, "Who do I turn to? How do I find a top 2 percenter in my lane or any possible lane?" Most importantly, how do you *experience* their knowledge in some way, shape, or form? Can you spend half a day with somebody? A day? A couple of days?

This approach is more valuable than taking courses. Go spend time with people. Ironically, self-education helps you figure out where you want to use your money on classes. Many programs aren't worth it, and a 2 percenter will tell you. Social media and the online world can broaden your horizons if used right. This allows you to find your lane without being encumbered by your surroundings, your past, or the expectations people put on you. But please, whenever possible, do this *in person*.

---

7   Basmo, "15 Statistics about Reading Books You Must Know in 2022," https://basmo. app/reading-statistics/.

My favorite three-letter word is *ask*. Say you're using social media to find and define your lane—that's the only reason for spending time on it—then don't be afraid to reach out to people. Direct message somebody to say, "Hey, I've been watching what you share. I've been seeing what you do. Can we schedule a time to talk?" If that person is three thousand miles away, it's virtual. But if they're within fifty miles driving distance, then by all means get in your car and drive. Buy them coffee, lunch, or dinner.

Broadening your horizons is about going places and meeting people. When seeking mentors, reach out and do something different from what everybody else does. Where most people just want to *take*, be the person who will give. Even mentors like to see their reflection in those they work with. The more you give, the more a great mentor will give back. Then, the mentor will be interested in helping you. Most days, I get fifty-plus requests from people asking, "Will you help me with this?" or "Will you help me with that?" or "How do I do this?"

Here's how you become a great mentee:

- *GIVE FIRST.*
- *BE FLEXIBLE.*
- *COME PREPARED.*

Often, people have done zero homework. Please, before you go to a possible mentor, do your research and know what you want to ask. Don't show up unprepared with "So, tell me how to do it all." Not interested. It takes too much time. The potential mentor knows you're not in your lane. You're not behaving like someone who is intentional and compelled.

When you're broadening your horizons and reaching out to those who can teach you more, show them you've done your homework and then prove you're willing to get in a car to make the interaction happen.

Make it convenient for the person you're asking mentorship from. Young people are guiltier than older people. I'll give you an example: "You can offer me wisdom! I'm free Tuesday from 8:00 p.m. till 11:00 p.m."

Well, good for you. That's not when I'm free, and if you'd like my help, you need to ask when I'm available. That's a pet peeve of mine.

Going back to the intentionality of social media, being intentional with your screen time and then having a process to introduce yourself to people is key. Realize that a top 2 percenter's time is exceptionally valuable. If you can show in the first thirty seconds that you're cognizant of that, and you're prepared, then you're primed to sit down with someone who can open worlds you're only dreaming about.

Get out into the world in any way you can. You have to get out there and look at it as an investment of time. Be willing to do this with zero dollars (coming to you) behind the effort. Everybody thinks they should be paid for every second of the day. That's not how this game of life works. If you want to get to your vision, if you want to propel your lane, you must be willing to invest time and money without a return. This proves that your lane holds value for you, which never goes unnoticed.

Let's return to the 80/20 principle. I see all these worlds out there. Everyone wants a side hustle or gig. If that side gig is a passion project, and you want that lane, do it. But if you're just trying to make a couple of extra bucks instead of getting great at your day job, then stop it. Go take more courses to be better at your job. Go spend that time with mentors to improve your performance.

If you don't like your day job and the gig is where your heart is, then lean in. Get into your lane and make sacrifices. Stop wasting time! Our time is precious and requires making fundamental decisions about the future.

- Go back and look at your yes list in chapter 3. Define how these yeses can broaden your horizons.

THE EVOLVING LANE

When I needed everyone to say yes, they said no. And when I no longer needed everyone to say yes, they all said yes.

The above is something I learned from the dental education pioneer L. D. Pankey.

If you're like most people, your day-in, day-out world can easily limit your experiences. When this happens, you simply succumb to any lane. If you're looking for advice, and you're willing to expand your physical world, then you can *discover and create* your lane. When you broaden your horizons, one of two amazing things will happen: you'll either find your lane or, in the process of working on your vision, you'll trip over something that you never expected and have an *aha* moment. Let's face it, the evolving lane is how some of the greatest discoveries were made.

Look at Starbucks for instance. In the beginning, they sold coffee beans and coffee-making equipment. Starbucks has evolved since then. Today, their coffee sales project a net worth of over $87 billion. The lane changed course. They tripped over it. Penicillin is another great example. Alexander Fleming didn't set out to invent the antibiotic. In 1928, he returned from a holiday to discover mold growing on a petri dish of bacteria. The mold seemed to inhibit other bacteria from growing around it. The self-defense chemical in that mold became penicillin, and even after this discovery, it took twenty years to perfect the medicine.

Defining your lane can lead to unimaginable discoveries. Great intent creates the potential for accidentally stumbling upon the next level of success. Your lane—the same as your perfect day, your vision, your big picture—is an evolution. Allow things to evolve. Don't be rigid. Be focused, but don't ignore the signs when something great leads you up a higher path.

This is where your mentors come into play. Talk out loud to them, and they may hear you having a conversation about something you tripped over. This is key. People glow when they talk about certain inspirations, and it often takes someone else to see the glow—"She talks about that more than she talks about the 'passion project'" and "He seems to keep drifting in that direction even though he says that's not what he wants," etc.

Getting personal now, consider finding the right person in your life—a component of bucket 1. *When* does it happen? When can you stop looking? I would argue that when you're inherently your best self and the pressure comes off, great things naturally happen. You're in your personal lane! The same goes from a business standpoint. When you're in your lane, attuned to your vision and thinking big picture, you increase the odds of something game changing falling into your lap. You're already on course, so then unexpected doors open.

Why does this happen naturally? Your lane is about self-discovery—it makes you happy, passionate, and energetic. As mentioned previously, saying *yes* in your lane opens you up to your greatest potential—goodness starts flying in your direction. Unplug the words "always" and "never." When you're focused, mentored, and in your lane, remain open to the progression, which you might not even see yet. Expect evolution.

We've discussed *yes* a lot, but there's a different kind of *yes*—you heard that correctly. In your lane, say *yes*, but hearing *yes* or *no* should make little difference. When you embrace your vision and believe in it, you can approach every scenario with this level of confidence and conviction: "I will give this my best, and if someone tells me *no*, it's okay. I don't need *yes*." This approach changes how others receive you—in person, on video, virtual handshake, or real. You are a different person when you are 100 percent comfortable in your skin with a *yes* or *no* reply.

Easier said than done, but I can't express enough the power of bringing your "I'm just going to put it out there" game. When you can walk into a room without needing a *yes*, then *yes* happens much more frequently, in personal and professional relationships. You're grounded in your lane—your authentic self.

- Below, I'd like you to imagine a scenario—an interview, pitch, or mentorship opportunity. Write down five reasons why yes isn't the most important outcome. Note your priorities in that particular situation and what it is about your big picture, your vision, that makes yes obsolete?

_____

_____

_____

_____

_____

FOMO—FEAR OF MISSING OUT

Joy comes to us in moments—ordinary moments. We risk missing out on joy when we get too busy chasing down the extraordinary.

—BRENÉ BROWN

The answer to FOMO—the fear of missing out—is, after all the broadening you've accomplished, narrowing your funnel.

At the beginning of your career, whether you're just starting or maybe trying to rediscover your path, it's best to have a large volume of interactions and test-drive them. Putting yourself out there and physically being in rooms with people is the simplest way to meet those who can advance your career—your vision—and to broaden your horizons.

Narrowing your funnel comes down to choosing what's worth your time.

In my Florida town, there might be ten different organizations I could be involved with. There are professional networking groups that encompass many different professions—some bring together, say, an attorney, an accountant, and a dentist—and a diversity of people in the same room in an effort to say, "Hey, my business can be complementary to yours. How do we help each other?" There are also organized dental groups. There's even a young dentist division. Along with these opportunities, there are community organizations I could get involved with. I'm a lover of art, and the Salvador Dalí Museum is right down the street—a great community to be a part of.

Meeting others is crucial, but as I narrow my funnel, I have to look at how many events these organizations are having per year. Also, how do I get there? How can I at least be a part of a group and support them when I don't have the time to attend an event? How do I connect without overly investing my time? You could argue that all of these membership opportunities are a professional investment because you're bound to meet others with common interests. Networking isn't exclusively beneficial to your professional career! You enrich yourself and build your people skills—you increase your value. Starting broad and narrowing the funnel requires assessing what you spend your time on and *who* you're spending it with. Which organizations do you love the most, and which would you be happy giving the most time to?

Don't be afraid to ask yourself which of these time investments *deliver.*

Maybe there's a chance to be in a room, be at a dinner table, or attend an event with people who expand your scope of thought. Perhaps they've built successful businesses or careers that are inspiring. Ideally, you might find a mentor. But as I've said, narrow it down.

Long term, it's unsustainable to be involved in ten organizations. No one can accept ten invitations in a week or have ten mentors (speaking in broad terms).

Broadening your horizons shouldn't lead to FOMO. Be selective after exploring as much as you can. Step back and ask yourself, "Of all these great people, who are the best? Who resonates the most with me? Who provides the greatest opportunity in terms of my personal growth? Which rooms have the people *you* can help and who can help you too?"

What are the interactions, mentorship opportunities, and networking events that are best aligned with your lane? Best aligned with your true self?

You'll gravitate toward situations where the people involved share your core values. Say you land on two organizations that are a perfect fit. You've narrowed the funnel and now commit on a deeper level. Whatever resonates with you, go *all in*.

Finding and defining your lane requires *deepening* it. Start wide and broad, make your choice, and then go deep. When you try to do too many things, you'll just be okay with a bunch of them. You'll never become the go-to person for any *one* amazing endeavor. Your niche needs to run deep, fueled by hard work, core values, mentorship, and dedication. Start with broadening, then end with deepening. FOMO helps you in the beginning and hinders you later. Once you define your lane, avoid the clutter and choose what propels you forward.

I remember being a little kid and living in a two-story house—not so unique. I'd be at the top of the stairs trying to hear what the adults were doing because I didn't want to go to sleep yet. Something great was going to happen! We never lose this part of us that fears missing out. That's why we involve ourselves in too many things—too much distraction. Whether it's networking or just having fun with friends, there's always that thought: this could be *the one*. The truth is that for every *one*, there are ten other options out there. Shelf it.

When I look at a CV or résumé with a hundred things someone has done, I assume that they believe it's impressive. But all I see is a padded résumé. Worse yet, someone who doesn't have a real interest in what they do. A *deepened* interest. They don't have a lane they truly care about. High achievers understand that a shorter list is more effective. The applicant committed to something. They broadened and then narrowed.

Value is gained where value is placed. Leaders seek out those who understand this principle. Two percenters talk to young people all the time when they're applying to a school, a program, or a job. The applicant is often in the mindset of, "I need to have all these things to show."

And on the other side of the table?

We're looking for signs that you've achieved things for the right reasons. You have your big picture and core values. You've defined a lane. Whether it's music, painting, gardening, or working for the community, the point is that the people on the other side of the table want to see that you've narrowed your funnel for the right reasons—your vision. You know yourself! And because of this self-awareness (the awareness this book instills in you), you put in the work.

Let's swing back to not needing *yes*—not needing to prove yourself. When you're in the room with someone who can help you, you don't need *yes*—or an endless résumé—because you *believe in* your lane. You're long-gaming it. Simply being in the room is a step closer to your big picture. As for the freelancer who quoted me at $5,000 an hour, she wasn't there to give; she was there to take. It wasn't genuine. Without commitment and consistency, there is no success. There's no other way to get from where you are to where you want to go—plain and simple.

Commitment—you're in your lane, devoted to the process, and consistent, and you follow through. You're either the person who lights up the room or lights it up when you leave. Do you know how you can light up a room? How to create energy and excitement around you? Integrity, patience, and devotion.

Discover yourself. Make decisions. Be in your lane.

- Write three interactions from this past year—dinners, classes, or events—that you attended due to FOMO.

_____

_____

_____

TAKEAWAYS

- If you don't define what you're known for, the world will define it for you.

- Devoting yourself to your lane allows your character to shine through.

- First, broaden your horizons and then narrow the funnel.

- Ditch FOMO. Which interactions help you?

- Less is more. Your résumé should show what you truly care about.

- You're either the person who lights up the room or who lights it up when you leave.

- Read more about "Defining Your Lane" at drdavidrice.com/resources and watch my video where I go into more detail.

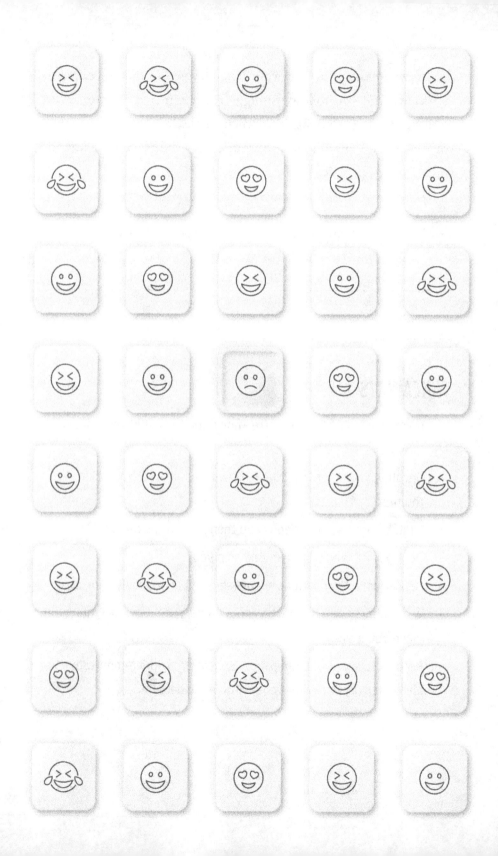

PART II

CULTURE BUILDING

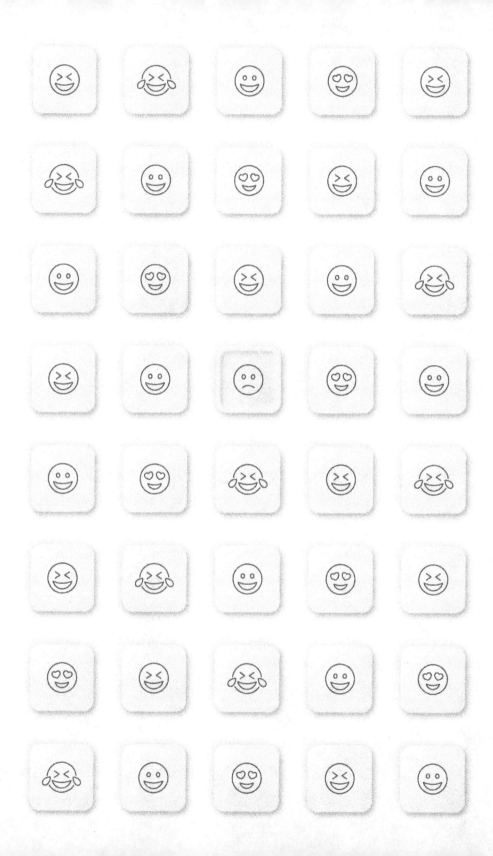

CHAPTER SIX

BUILDING YOUR TEAM

Teamwork begins by building trust. And the only way to do that is to overcome our need for invulnerability.

—PATRICK LENCIONI

Denny was a father figure to me who owned a women's headwear company in Buffalo. He did faux fur before faux fur was a thing, because for him it was a part of his core values. He was an animal lover. So it's my hometown of Buffalo—not very affluent—and Denny had maybe a hundred seamstresses who worked for him, which at the time was a piecemeal job.

The Wednesday before Thanksgiving, I was out of school and went to spend the day with Denny. I just wanted to see what he did, day in and day out. I watched everyone work until he offered this amazing Thanksgiving lunch. I was impressed by the camaraderie. After lunch, I sat with the secretary just outside of Denny's office. Out of the boss's door walks one of the seamstresses. She's crying, and immediately my head is spinning: "Oh my God, I thought he was a nice guy. He just fired her the day before Thanksgiving." I instantly went to a negative place. I don't know why, but I just did.

Adele, the eighty-something-year-old secretary, approached. "Do you have any idea what just happened in there?" she asked.

"Yeah, I think Denny fired somebody."

She shook her head and explained that he'd written a tuition check for the seamstress's daughter to cover her next semester in school, because she couldn't afford it. Adele added that no one would ever hear Denny admit to it. He did things like that all the time for everybody based on what they needed.

Years later, I wrote an article about him, detailing how impactful that moment had been. For me, it wasn't like I wanted to grow up to be a guy who ran a women's headwear company, but I knew *this is the kind of boss I want to be.*

Over a decade later, he called and asked how I knew about the tuition check.

"Adele told me."

He responded, "Why didn't you say anything?"

I went with my intuition. "Because I very much got the impression that, for you, it wasn't about looking good. You did it because you loved those people. You would've done anything for them."

Those who sewed hats in that business knew they could call Denny at two in the morning, and the boss would show up with tools to solve a problem and ask no questions. When he was needed, he arrived. He wasn't in his team's personal lives, but he showed up for things. They could count on him. This lesson was impactful for me.

Essentially, my greatest leadership and business lessons came from a man who sold women's hats. My greatest team-building model was Denny. Years later, a venture capital company came to him and said they wanted to buy Denny's whole business for $4 million. He said thanks but no thanks, because he knew if he gave over the company, they'd fire all those hardworking people Denny cared for.

He could have potentially been put out of business by those looking to buy. He knew that. He had a few years left—a few years left to take care of others. He didn't need the money. Denny didn't sacrifice anything. He was devoted to his team because his team was devoted to him. He chose strength and trust instead of making choices on a financial level. Denny could have fast-tracked it and taken that $4 million, then ridden off into the sunset. But he was okay with inching along because he was on track with the life he wanted to live. He did better than 99.99 percent of the world because he did the right thing all day, every day. Talk about a compelling, value-driven lane.

In this chapter, I'll discuss building a team—choosing your *who*. Building your team is very much about sticking with your vision and core values. Financial fulfillment meets personal fulfillment when you surround yourself with the right people—when you care about the people you're surrounded by. You select your team members and then invest in them.

IDENTIFYING WHO YOU WANT AROUND YOU

If everyone is moving forward together, then success takes care of itself.

—HENRY FORD

To put it bluntly, there are a lot of people in this world, and most of them shouldn't be on your team. Finding your team comes down to the same *narrowing the funnel* concept. In your personal life, identifying who should be on your team starts with your "nears," people who are close to you—they're in circles that are close to you already. You know who you want in your circle when something clicks! Like with anything important in life—your *where, what, why*—your *who* comes from a gut reaction.

When identifying these people, it's a great practice to have a folder on your computer—a page on your iPad if you're a notetaker—and compose a running list. This will help you organize *who* you are gravitating to. These are the awesome people you've met who could maybe be a good fit for your personal team. On a separate list, note who might be a great fit for your professional team. Put people you meet into two buckets. In the beginning, anything more than that gets complicated, and confusion sets in. But list the potential people and then start narrowing it down, because having too many people is as detrimental as having too many goals or too many career paths. Go with your gut.

Think of yourself as the CEO of your life. You're building your advisory board and board of directors. Your three mentors are the

> THINK OF YOURSELF AS THE CEO OF YOUR LIFE. YOU'RE BUILDING YOUR ADVISORY BOARD AND BOARD OF DIRECTORS.

most important people professionally, but if you want to add people to this advisory board, look for great people who already live the life you want to live, in some capacity. That's the simplest way of identifying those you gravitate to. Can they teach you something? Great! Then, *ask*. Invite people to spend time with you—those you admire. If you already know these individuals, spending time with them is easy. If you don't know them well, just be honest. Tell them they're someone you admire. Buy them lunch or coffee.

If it works and it clicks, ask if that person could be a mentor to you—or a friend. Ask if they're willing to help. If the answer is *yes*, then define how much time that is. Maybe meet with them once a month, maybe once a quarter. Sometimes, you meet people who are so cool you want to see them once a week. In your personal life, perhaps it's someone you want a lifetime with! Broadening your horizons and then narrowing the funnel helps you find truly great people, and with your list—not just a Facebook friends list—you have a catalog of those you can talk to and count on. This process naturally weeds out those who aren't serving you, but it requires thick skin. Don't feel bad if you meet someone who could help you, and they're just too busy for lunch. Don't feel bad if you go to lunch and they only had the time to meet once. Odds are, if you find a 2 percenter, they'll be busy.

Relationships are about trust. Both parties have to trust one another so no one feels taken advantage of over time. They'll just burn out. Understand that people give differently in any relationship. Both parties have to value what the other person brings. My example comes from my top priority in life. Sometimes, when I'm on the road and working like a crazy person, I think to myself, *This is insane. Anastasia gets to be at home.* In reality, Anastasia is the only person who makes our home click. She takes care of things so I'm able to do my work. If I didn't have her to help me, there's no way I could go do my thing, and vice versa. We couldn't have what we have if we weren't each doing what we do best. We ebb and flow, and we also give differently. This personal example also applies to your professional team.

I owned my dental practice with my colleague Mark. You learned about the impact he had on my life in chapter 1. It didn't stop there. Now, I was the highly engaged, social team member who went out and brought patients into the practice. I always outproduced Mark in the industry by fivefold. There was never a month when he approached what I achieved in that respect, because he was never the guy who wanted to go out and make all the connections. He was different. Mark was a steady, nine-to-five personality who did all the little things. He tended to the invisible, detailed stuff that I couldn't—and still can't—stand. I needed Mark's contribution to our relationship as much as he needed mine.

To set the record straight, Mark had just as much value as I did, and I couldn't do it without him. I tend to position myself as the person at the forefront. In that stance, it's easy to feel like you're carrying the whole damn load. Meanwhile, Mark was behind the scenes, not getting a lot of credit. That's when I learned that when you're the "face" or the "name" of a business, it's important to make sure every person on the team, even the quietest of people, gets all the recognition they deserve. Mark would never ask for it. He would never complain, but I know he needed it just as much as anyone else. When we recognize what others are giving and validate it, we invest in those who are vital to us.

- Begin your list of personal and professional contacts below. Who are the top ten in each category—those who click with you and have something to offer? If you prefer, compose this list on your computer or tablet.

CULTURE—THE *IT* FACTOR

Customers will never love a company until the employees love it first.

—SIMON SINEK

Being a values-driven leader impacts those around you. The leaders with heads on their shoulders are easy to spot. Like Denny. Authentic strength and leadership are clear. I would be willing to bet that with Denny's team—or my team over the years—there are moments when something you say or do is perceived as insignificant, not knowing what's going on in another team member's life behind the scenes.

Maybe a colleague lives with somebody who is never grateful, or never notices them—maybe they live with someone who nitpicks at every little thing they do, making them feel like they're constantly wrong. The full humanity of those we work with is never entirely visible. As a teammate or leader, if you reach out to someone and say, "When you did this, it was amazing," you feel great for catching a moment. But the person struggling behind the scenes might think, *I needed that today.*

Life is just as much about these simple acknowledgments as it is Denny writing a tuition check. These gestures are additive—contributing in small quantities to a collective big picture. In Steve Anderson and Walter Hailey's "Management: Seven Deadly Leadership Sins," sin 3 looks like this: "No recognition. This ranks as the biggest complaint team members have about their boss. All team members want to know how they are doing from the boss's perspective."[8]

Anderson and Hailey's work inspired me to write little appreciation notes during my workday. We write notes all day long, saying we

---

8   Steve Anderson and Walter Hailey, "Management: Seven Deadly Leadership Sins," Oral Health, June 2002, https://www.oralhealthgroup.com/features/management-seven-deadly-leadership-sins/.

appreciate one another. Today, it can be a text message or DM, but the notes are my favorite.

Pay attention to your culture. Find two or three people on your team and think of something encouraging to say. Notice something positive. When you do this, they pay it forward. The constant encouragement begins to stack up for a positive culture and strengthens your team, even outside the walls of your business. People realize that no matter their struggles in their personal lives, coming to work is pretty damn good. That's the kind of team I want to work with. I feel better when I'm surrounded by people who feel appreciated and supported, no matter what's going on for them behind the scenes. When your culture has this, when people feel better around you than when they're *not* around you, I don't care how many resignations there could potentially be—no one's going anywhere.

This is a big challenge today, and it likely applies to many professions. Seventy percent of dental offices can't find a dental assistant. Eighty percent have a hard time finding a dental hygienist. People ask me, "How's your practice?" Well, my team can't wait to come back to work. That's because we've crafted our culture for twenty years. There's no Band-Aid for this. If it's not working, start fresh. Clean off the wounds and start doing all the things you discussed months or years ago. Build it for the future of your next team.

Think about Chick-fil-A. Every teenage kid wants to go to work and sling chicken. Think about Google. How many employees go there and work for half of what they'd earn at the same job anywhere else? Google, Facebook, Instagram. When you have that *it* factor, the game gets a whole lot easier. That *it* factor is culture. With a positive culture—no matter how you angle it—you'll win. Everyone will win. If you don't, someone will take your team, because *valuing* your team—the people you click with and who inspire you—keeps those vital individuals in your corner. It creates well-being, as well.

- Who are three people you can encourage this week in some way, and how will this improve your culture in the workplace, school, or household?

_____

_____

_____

ACCOUNTABILITY

I think as a company, if you can get those two things right—having a clear direction on what you are trying to do and bringing in great people who can execute on the stuff—then you can do pretty well.

—MARK ZUCKERBERG

This quote from Mark Zuckerberg leads me to ask, "_Pretty_ well?"

As I'm writing this, Ignite is 99.9 percent a virtual team. There are times we're together in the same city, but in day-to-day reality, we're all over the map. We use Slack, as many companies do. We have channels for every project and team. Every Monday we have virtual team check-ins where everyone has a clear expectation. Every other week we have one-on-one calls with team members. They'll be asked if they're hitting their deadlines. Then, once a month, we do a Zoom face-to-face. Would it be better if we could do all this in person? Yes, that would be helpful.

That said, the look of teams has changed, but the definition is still the same. It's my job to set the vision so that, as a team, we are all clear on how to win. It's my duty to create accountability. Then, it's our collective job to collaborate and communicate so we consistently move forward together. Many are working remotely, but one-on-one is still the powerhouse because it's the best way to mastermind an idea share. One-on-one—virtual or in person—allows us to say, "You're doing an awesome job," but if something isn't going well, it's also a great place for us to give feedback.

Finding and defining your team brings us full circle to your core values, vision, and big picture. To hire someone new, you have to be clear about who this person is, what role they will fulfill, and what you need from them. Think relationships. I use what I like to call *The Dating Game* analogy. In the beginning, when everything is fresh, it's easy. We're all bringing our best selves to the table, so there's rarely pushback. But don't be complacent! *This* is the time to outline how to win the game, the time to set expectations/rules, and the time to define accountability.

If we wait until the honeymoon phase wears off, accountability may be misconstrued as punishment when it isn't—not at Ignite, at least. Our check-ins—the weekly virtual meetings, monthly team meetings when everyone is together, the one-on-ones—become opportunities to look at our markers. The markers and parameters are preset. These meetings are about seeing how someone is doing and where they're at with a project or milestone. If a project is due, we both know that it's due. If it's done before the meeting, then great! If it's not, we have an opportunity to find out why and a chance to pitch in and help if that's needed.

Sometimes things aren't getting done and bad work is repeated. In this situation, the Ignite accountability plan takes out the guesswork. I'd recommend that yours do the same.

Strike 1: We have a discussion, take a note.

Strike 2: We have a discussion, take a note.

Strike 3: It's not working.

The third strike means we're finished. It's not a question—it's not a discussion. There's never a fourth chance. It's time for us to part ways. It's not about anger, and you don't have to be mean. None of this suggests that a team member isn't a great person; they're just not a great fit. Reflexively, as a leader, maybe I'm a good person and not a good fit for you.

The first two steps of accountability are the most crucial and overlooked. Leaders love holding meetings. Often, they don't have agendas and nothing gets done, but they still love to have meetings. They never tell colleagues how to win and never have accountability on their side. This is an amorphous blob of wasting time. Listen, we're in a meeting for a reason—to help everyone around the table succeed.

It gives me peace knowing that my team is well versed in our accountability plan. When a team member strikes one, two, then three, it's never me being a bad person if I have to let them go. I'm just doing what we promised *each other* we'd do. This applies to me. If you work on my team and I'm not accomplishing things I'd promised, then you should call strike one, two, three, and fire me. Now, true accountability for a solid team? You'll rarely get to strike three more than once. Your best borderline team members watch your leadership and see you walking the talk. Your strongest team members observe and join you in holding others accountable.

This model is solid but brings up an important point: everything is always in flux. That's how the world works. Things are in motion. Nothing is ever complete. You never get to stop motivating or coaching. We need our teams to motivate us all the time. The same can be said for our mentors. Don't celebrate and proclaim, "I finished my mentorship!" Never stop learning from others. Mentors are our *core* team—but so are our partners, family members, and friends. You'll encounter many team members who play different roles along the path. They're not necessarily on your team for your entire life, but they're on your team for seasons.

Ideally, the core team stays the same, while others might come and go, getting you from A to B, B to C, and then C to D, etc. People will serve different functions throughout life, but there's no way to build core and seasonal teams if you don't have your vision buttoned up beforehand. Know your strengths and weaknesses before pulling in the role-playing team—the auxiliary team—because you don't benefit from ten more of *you*. You don't need a doppelgänger. You need those who are *not* you. Over time, you'll learn lessons from all these people—learn from their strengths, which are perhaps your weaknesses. You'll gain wisdom.

The *who*—the team you surround yourself with, the mentors, the loved ones—they have the power to guide you. Go broad, then narrow it down to find the right people. This process will change your life. It might seem overwhelming, and that's okay. Nothing worth achieving comes easily. It requires a new approach and lasting change.

TAKEAWAYS

- There are many people in this world, and most of them shouldn't be on your team—personally or professionally.
- Make a list of those who click with you, then narrow the funnel.
- Mentors, partners, friends, and family are part of your core team.
- Some team members are seasonal. They take you from A to B.
- Read "Build Your Own Team" at drdavidrice.com/resources and enjoy my discussion on finding those key players in your life.

CHAPTER SEVEN

CREATE LASTING CHANGE

Meaningful, lasting change only happens when the pain of the status quo finally outstrips the fear or the anticipated pain of the change we seek.

—DAVID TAYLOR-KLAUS

New habits are very difficult for people. I always think of New Year's resolutions and how quickly we can fall off the wagon. You've already read about some major changes I've made and how I'm a *throw-paint-on-the-wall* guy, but research does suggest that sustainable change starts with radical change. (Change is not the same as sprinting.) It's easy to make small changes in an unfocused way, but this gets old, tired, and boring. When you crave real change, you have to set a standard for what real change is for you. The big change has to be something *valuable*. Change requires intense conviction, preparation, focus, and vision.

Returning to your core values, if that big change isn't aligned with these, there's a good chance it won't happen. How does this radical change—goal or vision—drive the positive things you *want*, as opposed to simply eliminating what's *wrong*? There's a famous study by a cardiologist in Boston who measured patients and informed them of their poor eating habits. The test subjects were warned that they'd have another heart attack or die if they didn't change their diets. Patients followed orders but eventually drifted back to their former eating habits once their *fear* went away. Once, "Oh my gosh, this is going to kill me," wasn't in their heads, old habits prevailed.

In the study, many were fifty, sixty, or seventy years old—some had grandchildren—and so researchers tried a different approach. Patients involved in the study were reminded that they wanted to see their grandchildren grow, graduate, and marry and see all of the other milestones in life. The study proved that this positive vision for the future was the better method for enacting sustainable change. The truth is that lasting change has to begin with defining what is *truly* important to you—something futuristically driven.

Fear doesn't last as a motivator. The reason fear doesn't last is that we wake up and realize fears are usually unfounded. When nothing horrible happens, the inner script sounds like this: "I didn't have a heart attack yet from not exercising and not eating well," or "I don't have lung cancer from smoking," or "My quality of life has not gone down from the hours I spend on social media."

What positive vision for the future will create lasting change for you? How do you prioritize to maintain focus? You can try to change a lot of things at one time, and maybe you'll do okay at all of them. But if you focus, if you narrow in on your big change and bolster yourself with core values, the results will astound you.

This requires planning. It requires milestones and accountability. Set a date—what is the goal for that date? Make it realistic. I believe in assigning three actions to this new habit: two actions you know you will be able to handle, as well as one that forces you to stretch. Not a crazy stretch, but a stretch.

What new habit will make you better? What freedom and achievement do you seek from this new habit? New habits need to be (1) meaningful and (2) *sustainable*. Lasting change. It's not easy, but the work you put in deepens your ability to make the impossible possible for you.

- On the first line, write ten things you wish to change or improve in your life/career. Then number them in order of importance. These are all unique challenges, so start with number one.

_____

_____

_____

_____

_____

PLUGGING AWAY AT RADICAL CHANGE

Chains of habit are too light to be felt until they are too heavy to be broken.

—WARREN BUFFETT

Change without conviction leads to boredom, futility, and giving up, but lasting change comes from a *big* vision. Even radical change is slow. Say you want to lose ten pounds. That idea alone won't get you there, but having a picture on the wall from a time when you felt your best makes choosing between a candy bar and fruit a little more sustainable. You have a drive. Health, vitality, and freedom are perhaps core values for you. When these line up, your meaningful pursuit is no longer about deprivation.

At this point, you are working on your perfect day and filling in your scheduling blocks to reach your big picture. Take number one from the above list. How does that figure into your scheduling? Is it aligned with your core values? Does it fall into your personal, learning, or professional bucket? As you know, you block your perfect day because daily habits are helpful when you can't see the outcome yet. For most people, it's tough to envision even a month from now, let alone three months, six months, or even a year ahead. Having something to focus on every day that's doable leads to radical change in the long haul.

For some, this daily habit might just be a box to check. For others, it's a "feel good" motivation. With current technology, there's an app for pretty much every human goal, and these offer reminders. No matter what your radical change might be, if it's something you can do every day—if you can see it, feel it, touch it—then you wake up a month from now, three months from now, and realize, *Wow, I did take some pretty big steps closer to where I want to be with just these little action items.*

I say "plugging away" at radical change because, first of all, you have to, and second, everyone will create change at their own pace. At the end of the day, you'll get to where you're going in your lane, and there's no need to sprint. In the following section, we'll delve deeper into knowing yourself, but the fact of the matter is that some people are slow game changers and others need radical change to come quickly. Both approaches have the potential to be unsustainable, but both require *plugging away at it*—without knowing how fast it will go. I'll give a personal example.

A patient of mine who owned a gym was confident enough to comment, "Hey, you look like a guy who used to be in really good shape." *Damnit.* I knew he was right, and I'm glad he said it. Maybe he was just trying to get me to join his gym, but I was game. He had a machine that measured body fat, water, and muscle—the whole nine yards. He put me on that device and showed me where I was at physically.

I won't go into details, but needless to say, I didn't like the results.

An all-in approach doesn't mean it happens tomorrow. A lasting yet radical change can be a one-year goal for some, a two-year goal, or a ten-year goal. Knowing myself, I started throwing my paint on the wall. I worked out to the point of getting sick every time. That's how hard the trainer pushed me. I hated it. I felt awful. I just worked as hard as I possibly could for a whole hour until I was about to pass out. (I'm not endorsing this exercise method, by the way.)

My point is that I knew this about *myself*. If there's one big goal, I'm throwing myself headfirst into the pool. This was sustainable due to my vision, working with a 2 percenter, and knowing that I was getting to where I wanted to go quickly. The results I saw propelled me. If you need fast change, build your strategy based on that. If you need slow change, your strategy will make you just as successful. Know exactly who you are. The pace of your change is a part of knowing yourself. If you must sprint, do it after putting in the research and finding the right people to help you.

- Note three major changes you've made in your life—hard changes. Did these come fast or slow for you? What was the experience like? Past changes provide a lot of information in terms of what works and what doesn't.

_____

_____

_____

_____

_____

TO THINE OWN SELF BE TRUE

And it must follow, as the night the day, Thou
canst not then be false to any man.

—WILLIAM SHAKESPEARE

Change requires honesty. I don't want to come across as fatalistic, but not everybody's cut out for certain things. They're just not. That's a part of life. Otherwise, maybe everyone would be a rock star or brain surgeon. This isn't to say that making the impossible possible is false. It's to say that you have to know yourself and do the work. When you know yourself, you intuit your core values and your lane, and then achieving difficult things and enacting radical change is easier. You already know who you're working with. *You.*

When plugging away at radical change, be honest with yourself about what you're willing to do—what you're capable of. Radical honesty and accepting who you are take you much further than setting goals and never following through. That's why I mentioned the two reasonable action steps combined with the one that's a stretch. If you set a goal that isn't sustainable—perhaps you know from the get-go—then *not* following through each day will lead to the self-talk that we're all familiar with: "I can't do it" and "I can't get there" and "I've failed again."

Self-talk is vital. Looking in the mirror and being honest with yourself about what you can—and *will* do—is important. Listen, there will be changes you're not willing to commit to, so why waste your time and mental energy? Perhaps there's a goal you wish to accomplish in the future but just not right now. Commit to the things you *can* commit to right now—those aligned with your big picture.

The previous exercise was about narrowing the funnel in terms of where you want to put your efforts—this focus creates positive experiences, growth, and ultimately a sense of pride and accomplishment. Start with number one on your list, work methodically, and feel the residual pride that helps you to tackle numbers two, three, four, and so on.

As you know, I'm a big fan of looking back and assessing progress. Say you met that career/lifestyle/relationship goal—then you can assess the next step forward. After three to six months, perhaps you're ready to tackle something you weren't sure you were ready to tackle before. Maybe where you've come from and what you've achieved have increased your confidence and freed your focus for what you want next. One day, you'll find yourself on number ten or number twenty.

Knowing yourself and what you're capable of is empowering. I want you to be optimistic and futuristic—not in the *Star Trek* sense—but I also think people should be realistic and *to thine own selves be true*. I keep dangling the carrot in terms of chapter 8, but you'll come to learn that mentors are a big help in this effort. Your *who* can hold you accountable for what you're trying to accomplish, they can help you see yourself and what you're capable of, *and* they can tell you when to back off.

- Returning to your list of habits you'd like to change or create, note the goals that are realistic for you. Don't be afraid to cross things out completely. While you're at it, note those two realistic action steps for your number one goal and the one action step that is a bit of a stretch.

_____

_____

_____

_____

_____

CHANGE IN NUMBERS

It is the long history of humankind (and animal kind too) that those who learned to collaborate and improvise most effectively have prevailed.

—CHARLES DARWIN

Returning to my gym analogy, the trainer I worked with offered one-on-one time. There was always another trainer doing one-on-one, one-on-two, or even one-on-three sessions. So as hard as that radical change was for me, others were going through the same experience. Having a support system during any change is important. When it comes to knowing yourself, you might be competitive like me. I'm a competitive person! Having others around who were going through the same journey was a big deal—it pushed me further because, I have

> WHEN YOU SURROUND YOURSELF WITH OTHERS WHO ARE DRIVING THE SAME CHANGE YOU SEEK, WHEN YOU HAVE A SUPPORT SYSTEM, YOU'LL COLLECTIVELY DRIVE CHANGE IN EACH OTHER'S LIVES.

to admit, I couldn't allow someone who was a few years older to change faster. I couldn't have a younger buck than me change faster. Ego aside, everyone at the gym was feeling my pain, and I was feeling theirs.

When you surround yourself with others who are driving the same change you seek, when you have a support system, you'll collectively drive change in each other's lives. Talk about culture building. I was an adult who knew how to eat right and work out. Still, there was no way I could get the results I achieved without

(a) the community and (b) the trainer who was a top 2 percenter. A 40 percenter wouldn't have gotten me there. There wouldn't have been accountability had I not shown up at 6:30 a.m. Monday morning. In my experience, if I wasn't there getting ready at 6:25, the trainer would text: You're supposed to be here stretched and ready for 6:30, not walking in at 6:30.

When you *hope* to create lasting change, then sure, maybe you can do it by yourself, but radical change is bolstered by a team and culture that facilitates reaching your goals—plain and simple. The most difficult tasks in the world become less difficult when everyone around you is in the same boat—striving for the same things. You get to compare yourself, in a healthy way. Others encourage, challenge, support, and nurture the Mt. Everest you're climbing for.

Consider school. For me, dental school was pretty miserable, but it became less miserable because my peers were going through the same thing. So I studied with them, I worked with them, and importantly I had fun with them. Striving for anything in life is hard work, but it's the people you're surrounded by who will increase your chances. You carry one another.

- In terms of the number one on your list, who can help you to achieve this new habit? Also, is there a community that could offer support and meetups? Write down every idea you can think of to make this goal a reality. What is every option available to you? You need support! Don't be afraid to ask for it.

_____

_____

_____

_____

_____

EDUCATE YOURSELF ABOUT THE CHANGE YOU SEEK

Give me six hours to chop down a tree and I will
spend the first four sharpening the axe.

—ABRAHAM LINCOLN

At the beginning of any relationship, we tend to have exceptional habits. We listen well. We are radically curious. We do all the right things. Until we don't.

The Dating Game.

Good habits might be easy at first. We're driven by adrenaline, love, conviction—you name it—but you need to maintain these habits as time goes on. Lasting change requires a game plan. The football player Jerry Rice was famous for the "rookie mindset." He would show up to train with the 49ers every year, even after he was the best wide receiver in the NFL. Still, he'd show up with a rookie mindset. He'd try out for the team.

Without lasting change, there is no change. Consistency isn't possible without a foundation—a rookie mindset—since a solid foundation is key to every success you hope to achieve in this life. I use my McDonald's analogy. They don't make the best hamburger, but they sell billions of B-rated hamburgers every year. Why? They're consistent. If you're going on a road trip or traveling to another state or country, you might not prefer a McDonald's hamburger, but you know exactly what you're getting. That's why they're successful. Talk about a solid lane.

There's a social element involved in every lasting change. When you start something new, people will expect it from you. Whenever you raise the bar, people expect continuity. Quite frankly, stopping that new habit lets people down, especially when they were rooting for you. If a certain change wasn't realistic or sustainable—*to thine own self be true*—taking it on and then dropping it will lead to disappointment in the eyes of others. You must take the time to *decide* which habits you're going to adopt and think through how that change is possible in the long haul. If you're not willing to go *all in*—rapid or slow—then just don't add that yet. Or, as you've explored, perhaps not at all.

This is not to say that you should avoid important changes just because they seem too much. Many *necessary* changes can seem overwhelming. Give it the time, space, and pace that it deserves to be realistic. In the workplace, falling back on old habits shows a lack of commitment and leadership. Leaders tend to "fall off the wagon." This engenders an unpredictability that the human mind hates. People, for all the right reasons, decide they want to be better at something. In life, we get excited. We get emotionally involved, which is how we're all wired. We emotionally connect to an idea and then logically build all the reasons why that's a good thing to focus on. Often, something is missing.

Based on behavioral style, some people sprint right away without even thinking. Others emotionally engage themselves in what they want to achieve and do research to build a system for change. Then they go *all in*. With anything that you're striving for, there's almost always more to it than what you think. There's more to it than just reading a book or attending a lecture. There's more to it than what mentors have shared with you. Even mentors can simplify things for mentees, so they'll readily understand. So if you're only looking at one source, there's a good chance the information is simplified, and you've missed dotting the i's and crossing the t's.

Caution should be observed when emotionally connecting to something, somebody, or just a concept and then sprinting without identifying the places where you could fall. When you identify the places you can fall, you prepare solutions for falling. Sprinting without education, combined with no strategy, sets you up to let yourself and your team down. You're letting your customers down too. New habits—lasting change—require you to be fully informed about what you're doing. Bucket 2. Learn as much as you can from multiple sources. Further ahead, we'll discuss game plans and how examining best- and worst-case scenarios is so helpful.

HABITS AND LEADERSHIP

It's so important to have a genuine human regard for the people who work for you. To be a person of integrity, fight for people when they aren't in the room, and do what you say you're going to do.

—ARA TUCKER

Forming new habits as a leader is precarious when you're not *all in*. You have the potential to not only let yourself down but also your team. When designing your culture, lasting and enduring change is fundamental for everyone's level of confidence and enthusiasm. I mention falling off the wagon as a leader because it's so damaging. We've all been in that place where we think, *Joe or Jane has learned something new this week. Let's give it a month, and he/she will surely go back to business as usual.*

From a leadership standpoint, you can easily blow up your culture when your team knows you'll get excited about something, then run out of gas, and then it all goes away, again. Even in your personal life, people will start to wait it out and expect that, two weeks later, everything is "back to normal." As a leader, when this happens, no one will want to implement change because they know you will not sustain the change. Why should they bother? Why should they learn new things? Why should they work harder than they were working yesterday?

Why should those around you follow through with meaningful change in their lives if they see you step back?

Lasting change is difficult for everyone, but the pain increases when there's a team involved and it's not just you. The negative impact is more pronounced. Being a kid from Buffalo, I watched so many sports teams get ruined. Sure, they had all the talent in the world, and everybody came to see the game pumped and excited. Then the coach was crappy, or maybe the coach was pretty good, but the general manager was crappy. It doesn't matter how much talent you have if the culture is losing—when new habits and practices pass in the blink of an eye. In this case, the team isn't playing to win—they're playing *not to lose*. The challenge is that all the data shows that we cannot focus on the *opposite* of what we want and expect to achieve it. Playing not to lose translates into waiting to lose. You're waiting to fail—you've done it too many times. It's the precedent. There's no way out of this dynamic other than radical change—cleaning house—and that might mean that the leader who has to go is you or me.

Radical and lasting change is about fixing what is broken. No one will implement difficult change for the fun of it. Transformation begins with you, and it takes education, vision, core values, and strategy. Take the mirror test: if you're not passing your mirror test, you've got work to do, and this is propelled by honesty, introspection, and *vulnerability*. Vulnerability is a huge element in building new, bold habits. If you have a team that's looking to you, vulnerability and verbal skills will allow you to admit, "You know what, gang? All the bad stuff that's happened in the past, that's on me, and here's what I will do to change it. Are you open to change with me?"

And I don't mean to be dark, but if you have a personal habit that is bad for you, don't be afraid to reach out for help. Changing in numbers. Looking in the mirror and being honest with yourself.

Any path to lasting change must include accountability and milestones: month one, month two, and month three. A year. Get a small win, another win, then another. Define the new habits and state how you, and everyone else, will be held accountable. If it's a change you're making for yourself, reach out and find a community. If it's a leadership change, get your team involved.

Morale stays high when your *what*, *why*, and *who* are a part of your goal. Don't forget your *where*! Often, an important change needs to happen in the right place.

TAKEAWAYS

- Lasting change must be aligned with a larger vision for yourself.
- Change is not sustainable by negative reinforcement or fear.
- Prioritize the changes you want to make and begin with number one.
- Find a community for change. Find *who* can help you change.
- Research how to be *fully informed* of the change you seek.
- Keep learning at drdavidrice.com/resources with my blog "Building New Habits That Last," and the corresponding video where I go into a deeper discussion about lasting change.

CHAPTER EIGHT

THE CHEERLEADER, THE CONTRARIAN, AND THE 2 PERCENTER

Our chief want in life is somebody who will make us do what we can.

—RALPH WALDO EMERSON

This photo of me and Anastasia was posted on social media and received hundreds of likes and responses. As is the case with all social media photos, those who saw it probably assumed it happened effortlessly. The truth is that the snapshot was taken about twenty times from different angles, with different lighting, and finally with professional processing. This specific image was selected

because we're positioned in the right way to tell the very best story. My minute-and-a-half dental videos on YouTube look great, but they took hours of writing, rehearsals, takes, and edits to get them right.

This chapter is about mentorship, so you might be asking yourself how these things relate to one another. Well, this about *authentic* mentorship. The real deal. We are quick to seek out help in our careers, and often the flashy option catches our eye. What we see online are carefully staged snapshots and videos, so it's easy to get lost in those imaginary worlds. Everyone understands that we're all posting images or videos online that depict our very best selves, in the best possible moment. I cannot express enough how important mentorship is, but just as important as mentorship is finding the right mentors—real mentors. Specifically, *three* mentors. I'll explain.

When dentistry was all I was doing, something felt off. I hadn't found my *where*, *what*, and *why*. Equally as important, I hadn't found my *who*, until I saw those speakers on the stage. The day I started Ignite, I knew I was where I was supposed to be. I had no idea exactly how it would evolve, but the feeling of being "off" melted away. I was on track for something—I was en route to what felt like a calling. It also became clear that there were a lot of new skill sets I needed to learn, and this required mentorship.

I put my mentors into three buckets. One, you need a cheerleader. You need somebody who can pick you up whenever you're not willing to put in the work—when you're not excited about the work. When you feel like you won't make it or ask yourself, "Why am I doing this?" The cheerleader reminds you that you're good enough. You can do this! It's just a bad day or a bad moment. For this encouragement, you need the cheerleader.

You also need the contrarian.

The contrarian finds your blind spots. When the cheerleader is rooting you on, the contrarian is that little devil on your shoulder who says, "You're doing something that a thousand people tried, and it didn't work for those one thousand people. Is this a good idea? Are you that much better? Or maybe, do those one thousand people know something you haven't learned yet?"

Last but not least, the 2 percenter. As mentioned, this is a top-ranking professional in your chosen field. I coin this phrase from Brendon Burchard, whose book *Secrets of the Top 2%* highlights key traits of the most successful people on earth. One of the lessons struck me big time: "Model only the leaders." Find that top 2 percenter in your field and do whatever it takes to gain their knowledge—be an assistant or apprentice. Take their course and get to know them. If you can receive mentorship from the top 2 percenter, you'll get to where you need to go. Everyone else is a waste of your time. It's easy to look at someone you admire and say, "They were just born to do that." They weren't. They had help. *Real help.*

I love these three mentor buckets. When you're starting out, educating yourself, and reaching for mastery, your fastest road to success is to lock these three people down super soon. These figures might change as you evolve, but that's natural.

I know I made a mistake when I pretended to have all the answers early on. I thought that's what people wanted from me—to do it all myself.

People will respect you more when you reach out for help. And people *want* to help. In my head, I assumed that if I was going to be the best dentist, it was all on me. I went and took a bunch of courses and did all the research. Yes, I was driving hard, and this education and work ethic benefited me in the end, but I could have wasted less time if I'd been more vulnerable and just said, "Hey, *you* know what I don't know. Can you help me? What worked for you? What didn't work for you?"

Your impossible is possible. The vision you have for your life is attainable. But there's no need to muscle through it. There are others out there who already have the knowledge you're seeking. Take the time to find your cheerleader, contrarian, and 2 percenter. Reaching your goals in life is a collaboration.

To achieve this level of mentorship, you need the real deal. Not the salesman with the glossy website.

- Look over your list of contacts from chapter 6. Highlight any potential cheerleader, contrarian, or 2 percenter in the professional column. An interesting note, this can be done in your personal column as well.

REAL MENTORSHIP

If you want to bring a fundamental change in people's belief and behavior … you need to create a community around them, where those new beliefs can be practiced and expressed and nurtured.

—MALCOLM GLADWELL, *THE TIPPING POINT*

It frustrates me that we live in a world where an influencer gets paid to say everything they feel like saying instead of what's real and what's helpful. It will be a little bit of a dance because there *are* influencers who are excellent and have a strong message. I love some of them myself. But as I've said, with any major change or endeavor, taking the time to do your research is critical. Don't jump into something fast and throw your money away. There are bad people on social media. *Bad.* They don't care about you at all. I see hundreds if not thousands of people drinking their Kool-Aid—being led down the primrose path—but these folks won't authentically be in your corner, rooting you on, because that's not their intention from the beginning.

Let's be clear. To achieve what you want, you have to do the right things and interact with the right people. It's not true that you can be *anyone* you want to be. If you're over the age of fifty and want to start a career in the NBA, then let's be honest. I don't know how we draw a line in the sand here, but we *do* have to draw a line in the sand. Everything is possible when you take the right steps, you have a strategic plan, your timing is good, and you have the right mentors who can be honest with you. With your vision, big picture, blocked day, and buckets in order, *then* it is possible. But if you aren't working on these things, life will potentially not be as kind as you hope, simply because someone on Facebook told you it would be. They're selling you something.

Real, authentic mentorship ties a lot of this book together. One of the reasons I still practice dentistry is because I'd be a horrible dentist mentor if I didn't. If I talked about things I did ten years ago, they'd no longer apply today. Technology has changed. Materials have changed. People have changed. The world has changed. We now have what I refer to as "COVID kids"—their entire social, entertainment, and educational lives on a screen—as well as grown adults

> EVERYTHING IS POSSIBLE WHEN YOU TAKE THE RIGHT STEPS, YOU HAVE A STRATEGIC PLAN, YOUR TIMING IS GOOD, AND YOU HAVE THE RIGHT MENTORS WHO CAN BE HONEST WITH YOU.

who live in a virtual world. That's where relationships and communication are "found." But don't be deceived. This isn't real life moving forward. It's a piece of it, but it's not real life. Real mentorship—real connection—involves broadening your horizons and then narrowing your funnel to what's tangible and impactful for you.

When looking for a 2 percenter, find an authentic one. Who are the best of the best you want to learn from? The *authentic* ones, not the ones trying to sell you something. I'm talking about a 2 percenter not just in your profession but in your specific lane. Let's use law as an example. Say you want to grow up to be the best lawyer in the world. Okay, what kind of lawyer? Corporate, tax, personal, or perhaps injury? I'm not an attorney, but I know there are dozens of branches. So if you want to be the next trademark or patent attorney, then you need to have *that* person as your mentor. Not just a general attorney—they don't know anything about patents or trademarks. Maybe you find that 2 percenter and the dynamic is different. Perhaps that person could be your cheerleader because they went through it and know how hard it is. They naturally help you work through things with encouragement.

To clarify, a 2 percenter can fall into your cheerleader or contrarian category, but who you choose has to be specific. A core team member—someone who is willing to say, "I can take you from point A to point B, and after that I'll still be here for you." And although we want to lock these people in for life, this can still shift. The best mentors—the most open and vulnerable—are able to tell you when there's a better person to guide you to the next level. They began as your 2 percenter and stay on board to be the cheerleader, etc.

Any 2 percenter is so vital to your success, no matter your lane, because in this world knowledge gets diluted. When the best of the best teaches somebody who is pretty good, that student learns that the devil is in the details. The difference between pretty good and outrageously good might constitute thirty of the tiniest things. And if you miss any of those thirty little things, you'll just stay pretty good. That's where it stops. How do you learn those details if you don't have *access* to those details? Seek out the people who can take you from good to great. Why should your mentors be elite in what they do? Because more than ever before, we need to return to a paradigm of success and not failure.

THE NINTH-PLACE RIBBON

My great concern is not whether you have failed, but
whether you are content with your failure.

—ABRAHAM LINCOLN

Once you find an authentic 2 percenter in your lane, communication is key. It might sound like this: "Hey, I need your help. This is what I'm looking for. I want you to be honest with me. I'm the kind of person who might need you to soften my approach a bit." With the contrarian, you might need to say, "Shoot me straight. Don't beat around the bush. Don't tap-dance. Tell me how it is." Be sure your mentor is on board for what you're asking of them because, as I've already mentioned, if they're a 2 percenter, they're very busy. But you'll find that people who have accomplished much in life often want to help.

Gain permission and then define expectations. As a mentee, you should expect your mentor to have expectations of *you*. Show up having done whatever homework your mentor has requested. Arrive early every time and be ready, especially if this mentor is unpaid versus a mentor coach. That's a different kind of relationship, so be sure to do your homework before choosing them. Now, just because you're paying someone doesn't mean that they *can't* be a suitable mentor. You can't expect everything for free from people. If the interaction gets you off the launching pad, so be it, but in the grand scheme of things, a 2 percenter in any capacity is what you need.

You'll make mistakes. Having consistent mentorship guides you through these mistakes. Each mentor can play a different role when things go wrong and can prevent you from falling headfirst into a *cultural* pitfall. Here's the irony: the good part about life today is that we've come to a place where society accepts mistakes. That's the positive aspect of social media. "Hey, we all make mistakes!" The danger is landing in this modern culture where we *assume* we're supposed to make all our own mistakes and then learn from them. That's how you get from where you are to where you want to be, right? *Fail forward.* Yes, kind of, because some lessons you'll have to learn the hard way, and you'll fail. True.

Please understand that you could completely avoid many obstacles or failures when you learn certain lessons from your mentors instead of believing you need to learn everything yourself.

Instead of pushing forward without doing your homework, without consulting your mentors and your team, you're better off stopping and taking a breath. *Consult people.* If you have broadened your horizons, narrowed your funnel, and chosen the people who you know can truly help you, then lean on them. What you'll find is that probably 70 percent of the mistakes you potentially would've made, you won't have to make. Mentors have already made them and can show you where things go wrong *before* they go wrong or after they *went* wrong.

Here is the plus-minus of where we're at today. The cultural pitfall. It's okay to talk about mistakes, which is great! But I would suggest that "I get better by failing" is not always relevant. That blanket statement has no nuance. We get better by little failures, yes. But a culture that actively flaunts failure makes it acceptable for people to not seek out authentic guidance and cultivate new habits.

We award kids the "ninth-place ribbon." It's misleading to hand out awards for fourth place and after. Listen, it doesn't make you a bad person if you didn't place. It just means three people did a better job. There were three more qualified people. The *everyone gets a trophy* moment in our culture might make people feel good for a time, but it's not inspiring the rigorous work required to push ourselves to learn and grow.

To put this damaging culture shift into context, let's look to the culture that preceded it. There's a fine line. We used to be upset with people, *angry* at people, and we made kids feel bad when they didn't win. That was a bad lesson. But an equally bad lesson is to hug your kid and tell them losing every day is good. It's not good—it's *trying*. I believe a better lesson would be, "You didn't make it today. Let's sit back and figure out how we can make it better next time. And if you don't make it better next time, it's still okay. We can figure out how to get better." Or maybe it's just not a valuable pursuit. I understand if readers are sensitive to hearing this, but *let's go get (feel better) ice cream because you lost by a hundred points* is as detrimental to kids as making them feel *bad* for losing by those one hundred points.

We're culturally rebounded from an unhealthy approach to failure, but we've swung in the opposite extreme. No more ninth-place ribbons. This doesn't encourage growth or finding the mentorship you need. If you lost by a hundred points, find someone who used to lose by a hundred points, and now they always win.

HONESTY AND VULNERABILITY

The delicate balance of mentoring someone is not creating them in your own image, but giving them the opportunity to create themselves.

–STEVEN SPIELBERG

The contrarian is the hardest mentor to find because we naturally want people to tell us we are on track—that we're right. "Life is going to be fine, and you'll do all the right things." Early on, we all have a contrarian in our lives. We have that friend or family member who has the opposite perspective. We tell them it's a beautiful day, and they find a cloud. We tell them it's a cloudy day, and they find a blue sky. Please don't misconstrue the contrarian as being a pessimist. We don't want someone negative, but we *do* want someone who sees the opposite of what we see. That's the contrarian in a nutshell.

Be intentional in searching for your contrarian because it's vital to have someone who looks at things differently. From the business and professional side, it's a great lesson to see how others who are different from you think, make decisions, and act. When you identify any style or approach that is foreign to your personality, that's your contrarian. If you're a quick decision maker, you need to find someone who's slow and steady. If you're an outgoing person, then you need someone who is hyperanalytical. This also works vice versa. If you're hyperanalytical, find someone who's social and gets along with people. If you're chill, you better find someone who knows how to make quick decisions. These opposites work great together.

I come back to my former partner, Mark. Our personalities were so different. In the beginning, when we were learning so much, we said to ourselves, "The other guy doesn't know what he's talking about. I wish he was more like me." As we invested more time and educated ourselves, we realized that the other person had skill sets that came naturally to them and were difficult for the other to achieve. You can try to learn something on your own, or you can allow your contrarian mentor to teach you those skills. Over time, you see the value in what the contrarian brings. This is not only a mentor—this person is your double-check. From Mark, I learned how to be more analytical. I learned how to take a step back and take a breath. He helped me to become a better leader, partner, and person. So we helped each other.

It might seem hard to have someone tell it to you straight, prove you wrong, or uncover one of your weaknesses. But in the business world, if you simply want to feel good, that's fine, but wouldn't you rather *do* good? Wouldn't you rather improve? Mentors help you perform better and get a little closer. That's something to be proud of because I don't know that there is a finish line. When you're driven, you achieve, and then you set a new finish line. Therein lies the need for balance—keep the finish line moving forward while taking time to stop and celebrate the wins.

Before we end our discussion on mentorship, it's important to be honest with yourself. There are many reasons why any great mentor might not be the best fit for you. First and foremost, they have to be *willing*—they have to want to do it. Second, on top of wanting to do it, they have to be able to create the time to commit to you. If you prefer a slower pace, it will be easier to find mentors because you won't need them as frequently as somebody who wants to accomplish fifty-plus things. That person might need their mentor every single week.

Another scenario is that you might be a mentee to a 2 percenter and then *you surpass them with time*. They took you from A to B. They passed the baton. Now they're your cheerleader or contrarian, or it's time for the arrangement to become a friendship. The dance of mentorship means that you might need to reevaluate and course correct as time goes on, adding someone new to your team. Last but not least, you will have to move on from a mentor when the dynamic simply doesn't work.

Things happen. Somebody could commit to you today and be the right person, but who knows what will come along in their life or yours. Date before you fall in love. In terms of personal relationships, don't fall in love with someone thinking they'll be the very best until you know that they *are* the best, and also that it will *work*. Then it's okay to dive into the deep end. Flipping back to the professional side, questions and conversations will give you a gut reaction as to who should be on your team—a team where mentors are essential. Find authentic, honest mentorship. And also, be honest with yourself. Are you working with the real deal, and are you open to the hard truths they can share with you?

As we're about to discuss, you need the cheerleader, contrarian, and 2 percenter in your corner when venturing into the unknown.

- Who's your cheerleader right now? Who's your contrarian? And if you have a 2 percenter, write down how each of these have moved you ahead.

_____

_____

_____

_____

_____

_____

_____

_____

TAKEAWAYS

- Your cheerleader, contrarian, and 2 percenter play different but vital roles.
- Be aware of "mentors" on social media. They're often trying to sell you something.
- Ditch the "ninth-place ribbon" mentality.
- Be open to criticism. Mentorship requires authenticity and vulnerability on both sides.
- I delve deeper at drdavidrice.com/resources with "Mentors: The Cheerleader vs. the Contrarian—Why You Need Both," as well as a new video on mentorship. The QR code will take you there too.

CHAPTER NINE

VENTURING INTO THE UNKNOWN

Until you step into the unknown, you don't know what you're made of.

—ROY T. BENNETT

In chapter 4, I told you about my best friend and having to make the difficult decision to set that friendship aside for my own best interests. It was one of the hardest things I've ever done. We had a fantastic time together, but I needed to grow.

An even more difficult decision was leaving my dental practice in Buffalo. It would've been easier to stay in a business that was doing well. I had a great team, firing on all cylinders. Not that we didn't have our hiccups, but we'd built a solid machine, and everyone was on point. We worked so hard to do the right things daily. Our team took a lot of lessons from this book—before it was written, of course. I'd built that practice, and part of me loved it, but another part knew it wasn't my last stop.

There was something bigger for me out there, so I had to take a giant leap of faith. These lessons will undoubtedly take you somewhere new as well—into the unknown.

I had to sit down with my colleague Mark and admit that the practice wouldn't be my final destination. The day would come when I'd need to move on. But getting from that conversation to the moment of, "Okay, here we go. The next chapter is starting," took a long time. It was emotionally liberating to arrive at that spot and, as you can imagine, very challenging. Throughout this prolonged transition, I was slowly getting out of my comfort zone because I knew I'd have to learn many new skill sets.

By the time I was ready to take the leap, I had already become a public speaker. You'll recall my first attempts at this and how I felt like a fish out of water. So I put work into developing that talent during the transition, and it was in my wheelhouse—in my world—by the time I was ready to leap. When it came to the dream phase of Ignite, I knew nothing about social media or building websites and online communities. I was more of a role player—some big meeting in New York, Chicago, Boston, or California would bring me in to speak. It was within my comfort zone at this stage to just walk in and do my thing. With Ignite, I had no idea how to build on that—create new events every week, even bigger events every quarter, and anything else for that matter! These challenges were all shockingly fun, exciting, exhilarating, and just outright frightening.

Ironically, I started Ignite precisely where this book starts— finding my *where, what, why,* and *who.* Then, I began with a concept, an idea, and a vision. I reached out to my 2 percenter mentor, Steve Anderson, for guidance. I hoped to fly out to Texas to sit down and discuss things. Talk about venturing into the unknown! I was willing to fly out of state to hash out a dream that was simply in my mind but, more importantly, a part of my big picture.

TAKE A LEAP OF FAITH

*As you struggle through whatever you are going through, remember
there is help somewhere, someone out there has solutions, and you
will stumble upon them when you take action to break away from
the old and have a steadfast, bold approach towards the new.*

—GERMANY KENT

I had other mentors at this time, but Steve was the guy I'd made myself
vulnerable to, saying, "I have this crazy idea. If I fly to Fort Worth,
would you spend half a day with me? I need to talk out loud and have
you tell me if I'm out of my mind—or onto something." I wanted to
know where my blind spots were, and Steve would be honest.

Even though I had people cheering me on, I needed my 2
percenter, and as we've discussed, with any important mentor, I
wanted to make it worth his time. The plan was to do my homework,
book the flight, and get to Dallas—all these steps made it easy for
him to say *yes*. As it turned out, he blocked his entire afternoon and
picked me up at the airport. We went to lunch and spent three and a
half hours discussing questions like:

- *"IS IT A GOOD IDEA?"*
- *"HOW DO I SHAPE IT?"*
- *"WHERE DO I GO?"*
- *"WHAT DO I DO?"*
- *"WHO CAN HELP ALONG THE WAY?"*

That last one is a biggie. *Who* are the people I need to help make
it happen, and also, what are the first steps? As you can see, in the
process of letting go of my practice, I was crafting a new vision for
the future. Not just dreaming about it—*working* on it.

Steve's advice was crucial and inspired me to find my *who*—a new core team. I talked to friends and got referrals to those who knew how to build websites or who mastered other skills I didn't possess. Keep in mind that I was finally at a point in my career where I *could* outsource. When starting from scratch, it's valuable to learn everything yourself until you can hire others. As we'll touch upon in chapter 11, these employees aren't leeching money from you—they're adding to your value.

Once the moving parts were in place, I had to take a leap of faith and let go. And in the face of doubt, I asked myself my favorite questions: "Why not me? Why not now?"

Sometimes, you have to look around at other people and say, "Well, if *they* can build something new, why can't I?" I knew I had to work hard. I had to study. There were so many things I'd have to face, but if I did, why couldn't *I* be successful? Stop worrying about what will make you fail and, instead, focus on what will set you up to succeed. Even with great advice, it will take twice as long as you think—maybe three times as long.

- Write down your wildest dream. Now, who do you respect enough to share your wildest dream with? If it's a 2 percenter, note how you can make it worth their time.

_____

_____

_____

_____

_____

_____

_____

_____

DON'T FEAR THE WORST-CASE SCENARIO

One thing that makes it possible to be an optimist is if you have a contingency plan for when all hell breaks loose.

—RANDY PAUSCH

In my mind, I always play the best- and worst-case scenarios. We have to be aware of the former and the latter. Steve could have shared that it was a great, average, or bad idea. Happily, he thought it was a great idea, but I still had to consider my worst-case scenarios. There were two: "Well, if this does absolutely nothing, then it could be a great giveback to the industry." Also, "If I fall flat, I still have my degree in dentistry. I could return and do something different in the practice space or in education."

In essence, I had my plans A, B, and C lined up, just in case. But plan A was the vision. I put all my energy and focus into it because I'm a firm believer that if you *don't* throw everything into plan A, then you probably won't get plan A. I wanted success, but if I didn't succeed, it wouldn't be the end of the world. I had both sides of the coin figured out. Sure, it might *emotionally* break me if the plan failed. It might set me back a couple of years financially. But it wouldn't *break me* break me. I had options. Once I knew that, I went with my gut—and Steve's guidance. I tabled everything outside of plan A and organized precisely how this leap of faith needed to play out to work.

In essence, a leap of faith isn't a blind leap. Venturing into the unknown requires preparation and a safety net. I knew where I wanted Ignite to go directionally but not exactly how we would get there. I was flexible enough to reason with my team. "Let's focus on these three things. If one of these accelerates our path, we'll do a lot more of that. If one of them yields nothing, we'll drop it and replace it with something else." We had a good mixture of courage, expertise, risk-taking, and data. We had balance.

Some people either don't get locked in enough—they don't fully commit—or they go to the other extreme and overlock. They're not adequately flexible to change when things aren't going well. There's a book I love titled *Three Feet from Gold*, by Greg S. Reid and Sharon Lechter. The story goes like this: A guy buys a bunch of equipment to mine for gold. He spends his life savings—his *family's* life savings—then runs out of money and quits mining. As it turns out, somebody else grabs his mining equipment and digs three more feet away, where they strike it rich.

This lesson is about *not yet* striking gold. Push through these moments because you might figuratively be three feet away from your goal. But there's something unseen underneath the message. I can't help but look at this analogy without thinking about mentors. What if the gold miner had been better informed? What if he needed to be more flexible and adjust his approach to discover what awaited him steps away? Sometimes, you simply need input. It's funny because many read *Three Feet from Gold* and think, *Oh, if he'd just dug three more feet!* But if he was digging three more feet in the wrong *direction*, it wouldn't have made a bit of difference.

Plugging this further into our mentorship model, the cheerleader would tell the miner he could do it! The top 2 percenter could help him find the best location and equipment. Then, the contrarian would say, "What if you're three feet away, but you're digging south instead of north?"

Account for all of the possibilities. When choosing your path—or switching gears—figure out all the angles and understand them. Get the mentorship you need. Once trusted mentorship gives you the green light, go *all in*. When you are informed and committed to the best-case scenario, you'll get to your plan A.

- Go back to your wildest dream—your plan A. Beside it, write two worst-case scenarios, and beside them, imagine your plans B and C.

MAN, THAT'S HARSH

Harsh ways are taught by harshness.

 —SOPHOCLES

Any leap of faith is met by both encouragement and backlash. When I was leaving my practice, some commented, "You're crazy. You have this great practice. What are you doing?" I think they resented my departure. Others were quiet and didn't share. Then, there was a group of people who found the prospect exciting. They thought it was cool! You have to listen to your inner voice and know what's right for you, because you'll hear all the good, the bad, and the ugly.

My family and core group of friends from Buffalo thought I was insane. Those connected to the world of my practice were hurt. The sentiment was, "Wait a second. We've been building this *we-before-me* model for twenty years, and now you're going to bolt?" Initially, they never thought I'd actually carry out my vision. They assumed I was talking out loud.

When it comes to the naysayers—and I'm not referring to mentors who offer informed discouragement—I think you have to deal with it. People will be hurt when you make any big change. Be open, honest, and communicate well enough in advance. As I've mentioned, I'd shared with my team that I wouldn't be present forever, and my phaseout happened over time. I certainly didn't sprint. I got all my ducks in a row, so by the time I truly walked out the door, it had been ten years since we'd talked about it. I didn't want it to be a surprise for them or to place my patients in an unfair position, but I also knew what I wanted out of life. It just had to be.

Many fear the backlash when they venture into the unknown toward their vision. But my opinion is this: you can't stop the train. The inevitability is the awesome part. If you've invested time in yourself and figured out your perfect day—which moves you to the big picture— then you've *emotionally connected* to the journey ahead. Once you are, you can't stop the train. You've already committed. For most, once we emotionally commit to something, it's just a matter of time, and during that time it's vital to remain consistent using strategy and intentionality.

Your emotional drive will inspire you to work, research, and find those mentors. These are the board of directors who can help you. Plan the process for what you want. A dream will not come together on its own. Your focus and flexibility on the road to that dream will tie it all together.

I use my car analogy. You decide that you're going to buy a certain car. You've done the research, and now you *seriously* want this car. Perhaps you have the money, but maybe you'll wait. You go for a test drive, and *you're toast*. We all have these things pulling us. For some, it's a car. For others, it's moving to a new *where*. Maybe it's clothes or technology. Once you're on Amazon and start looking at something you sincerely want, you'll get it. Our inclination toward *change* is similar. You have that deep desire, and you can't make it go away.

I'm not telling you that starting a new career is the same as buying a new pair of jeans online, but *emotion* is behind these movements in life. You won't be able to stop the momentum, and that's a great place to be! Specific visions pop into your head, and if you don't follow through on them, you wake up one day and ask, "Why didn't I go for it? Why didn't I try?"

You'll receive criticism while pursuing your vision. There will be rejection. But look at what Steve Jobs has to say: "I have a great respect for incremental improvement, and I've done that sort of thing in my life, but I've always been attracted to the more revolutionary changes. I don't know why. Because they're harder. They're much more stressful emotionally. And you usually go through a period where everybody tells you that you've completely failed."

VENTURING INTO THE UNKNOWN AS A TEAM

Change is the only constant.

—HERACLITUS

We've discussed personal leaps, but what happens when amazing people join your team along the way? Developing a culture that expects innovation from one another requires a certain mindset. Mindset propels both individuals and companies. What is your culture mindset? What are you collectively cultivating? Where are you leaping together? I've mentioned that I don't watch the news. Anything you feed on that is negative or takes away from the mentality of, "I can do this. Why not me? I will succeed," will interfere. Eliminate it. Be mindful of what contributes to your positive mindset and what doesn't—the same goes for the people who surround you.

Your team's mindset should align for a collective vision of excellence—venturing into the unknown. From a leadership standpoint, if you don't believe you will win, no one else will. They can't.

I didn't know I could achieve anything when I was a kid. I didn't have a mindset that could propel me into the unknown. Now, I truly understand that there's nothing I can't accomplish—it just depends on what I want. I don't believe there's anything out there I can't do when it's simply a matter of learning a skill set and deciding if it's for me. This is a core value—a core *understanding*. In terms of a team, this mindset is contagious. It makes it easier for everyone at Ignite because these young people dive right in. They know everything is possible.

I return to the worst quote on earth: "Children should be seen and not heard," a relic of my childhood. If you've received these terrible words, you know that they make you feel insignificant in the world. It's the opposite of affirmation. I'm telling you, not only can you be in control of *your* world, but you can also be in control of the world around you. We create our world in many ways.

The unknown requires courage, but it mainly involves conviction and hard work. There will be naysayers and criticism, but with the intense focus you're putting into your lane, none of these matter. Get mentored and coached, hold onto your values, and know that the unknown has incredible gifts waiting for you, thanks to your efforts. Your vision is propelling you as you build this infrastructure. You can't venture into the unknown without everything you're learning in this book.

As we dive into part III, I'd like you to return to where you started. When you feel stuck, reflect upon your perfect day. In fact, constantly step back and reassess what you're working on and where you want that work to take you.

- Just for fun, note the elements still taking up your time that are not a part of your perfect day. Why do these actions make you unhappy, and how can you eliminate them? So much of venturing into the unknown is letting go of what's holding you down.

_____

_____

_____

_____

_____

_____

_____

_____

_____

_____

_____

TAKEAWAYS

- When focusing on your vision, explore the best- and worst-case scenarios.
- People can be harsh, because many hate when others change.
- Venturing into the unknown is a growth mindset.
- A leap of faith is possible for an individual or team.
- Be informed and flexible during any great effort.
- You know the drill. Head to drdavidrice.com/resources for "The Power of the Unknown," and check out the video.

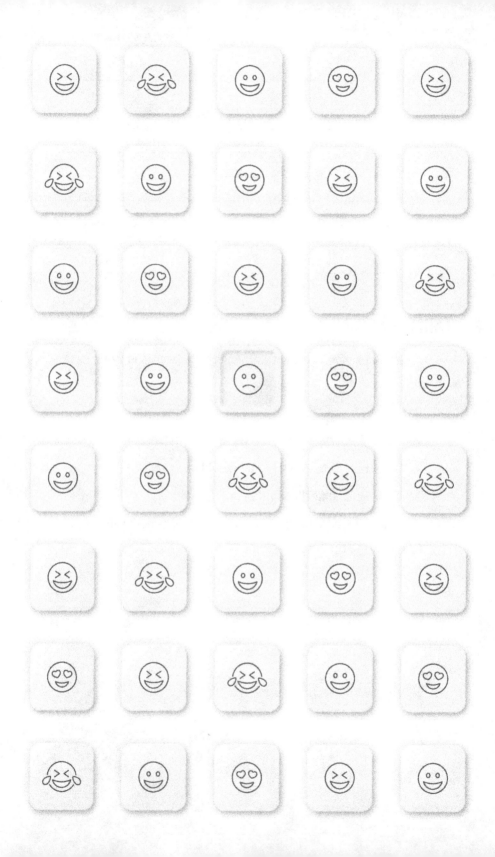

PART III

YOUR PERSONAL WORTH

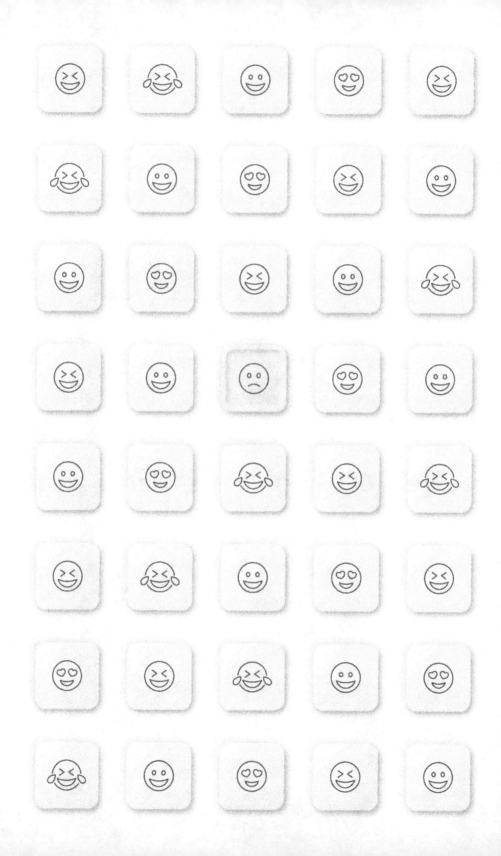

CHAPTER TEN

THE VALUE YOU BRING

The secret of joy in work is contained in one word—excellence.
To know how to do something well is to enjoy it.

—PEARL S. BUCK

The word "value" can be triggering for some. Yes, you were all born with tremendous value. Surround yourself with people who love you in your personal life, no matter what. We're all created equal. But in your professional life, it's just not true. We aren't created equal. We all have a number over our heads—a value. Some of that value comes from job position, and there's a value limit based on that position. Our ability to grow our value is what defines our professional success in life. There's a range in the dental world—the dentist, the hygienist, the dental assistant, and the business admin. There are ceilings of value for each of these.

> *OUR ABILITY TO GROW OUR VALUE IS WHAT DEFINES OUR PROFESSIONAL SUCCESS IN LIFE.*

If you can get out of your box and learn to create more value, then the sky's the limit.

So how do you raise your number? Aim to be five times your perceived value to anyone you do business with. If I'm worth a thousand bucks an hour, I'll give you five thousand in value—an excellent minimum exponential that few understand. You're stalling yourself when you think, *If you give me a dollar, I'll give you a dollar's worth of work, and that's great.* Well, sorry, that just makes you a friendly employee, but it doesn't allow you to raise your number. Two times or three times the value isn't enough. Five times is what you must deliver to get ahead.

This number might startle you. How do you accomplish that in your current space? Sometimes, it's purely dollars and cents. If I have a product, then you help me sell five times more than what you charge. In the marketing world, it's brand awareness. How do you blow up a brand for someone so their team can realize five-plus times the return on investment?

We're talking data, but the other end of the equation is character. You don't just raise your value by earning income—you also increase it by being the calm in the storm. You raise your value by being that go-to person whether it's a small, medium, or large company. The more you can plug yourself in and run the whole show, the more you're worth. Creating calm *and* running your end of the show is worth a lot of money. Deescalating drama is worth a lot of money. These traits create as much value as *making* money.

Growing businesses and being a problem solver are also immensely valuable. In my leadership position at Ignite, I've come to an understanding. Anyone who allows me to unplug, meet up, and say, "Tell me all the great things that are happening," and "Tell me what you need help with," and "Great, I'll see you next week," etc., proves that

that individual is tremendously valuable. When I need to inject myself into a situation and act as the problem solver, the peacemaker, the one who drives growth or manages minutia, that's a red flag for me.

The value you accrue is a lifelong process, so let's begin at the beginning.

THE VALUE OF EDUCATION

A human being is not attaining his full heights until he is educated.

—HORACE MANN

Your time investment in the learning bucket leads to knowledge. Knowledge will provoke you to broaden your horizons so that you encounter new people and experiences. Where do all these components naturally come together?

Attending a college, university, or vocational school not only provides you with proficiency, but it also offers opportunities for social connection and networking. The longer I went to school, the more I developed as a person. It's funny how society expects kids to learn in high school. You're too awkward to figure most things out, so you sort of wade your way through. Once you get to undergrad, you're thinking, *Okay, I'm technically an adult—or at least I'm proclaiming to be an adult*, so you have the breathing space to develop new skills. If you make it to a postgraduate education, many more layers are discovered.

Knowledge comes once you settle into yourself and *learn how you learn*—the greatest lesson—which comes to each of us at a different pace. I recall my second year of dental school, waking up one day and realizing I knew how to learn! I could now take in lessons at an accelerated pace because I'd figured myself out. I'm sure some people figured themselves out faster than I did, but suddenly I could handle any information that came to me and process it logically. I could digest, categorize, and draw upon it when needed. Equally important—I could foresee the next chunk of information coming my way. You have to be clearheaded to do any of this.

Whether we like it or not, the number on our heads goes up as we further our education. Some of this is formal education, and some is self-study and apprenticeship. All of these are valuable. If I were an electrician or plumber, I would get the education I needed and then apprentice a top 2 percenter. Combined with the right work ethic and stable personal life, I would be bound for success. But it wouldn't stop there. I'd continue to educate myself on running a business—how to lead a team. I'd take courses in management and marketing and keep adding these layers until my value increased exponentially. Most people can manage their piece of the puzzle, but what's the extension of that? Where can it go? If you're looking to pivot or build upon what you're doing now, you'll need further education and mentorship. You'll need to dream bigger.

In the early stages of education, it's all about learning for learning's sake, which helps the brain develop and grasp problem-solving skills. This development is a minimum requirement for value, but it's not the end of your story. Keep progressing! I went to school to be a dentist, but very little of what I do at Ignite has anything to do with dentistry. Companies call upon me because they're seeking all the skills I talk about in this book. I never stop learning and growing. Many people have a narrow focus, only knowing what's within the four walls that surround them. They get lost in minutia. If this has happened, and you wish to increase your value, it's time to have that vision, education, and mentorship to pull you up to the next level.

YOUR LAUNCHING PAD TO VALUE

Every moment of one's existence, one is growing
into more or retreating into less.

—NORMAN MAILER

Getting out into the world and attaining a higher level of education brings life experience, which makes you more valuable. Any education you spend time and money on raises the value on your head. Why do educational institutions make you more valuable? They force you to learn how you learn while *enhancing your social skills.* There's also greater expectation put upon you. It seems daunting. Once you climb to a new level in the educational process, somebody says, "It's not fifteen credits this semester—it's nineteen." Then, "No, it's not nineteen—let's do twenty-five. Oh, in addition to twenty-five, let's have these writing labs as well as *X, Y,* and *Z* that you need to be a part of."

Although stressful, this system pushes you out of your comfort zone and forces you to learn quickly and effectively—to balance your time better. You need to figure yourself out. You're building a muscle. There are only so many hours, and you need to eat, sleep, and have fun in the process. If you want to take care of the necessities of life—and fun *is* one of them—you must learn to manage yourself. Self-management is a fundamental part of the experience.

In college, your room is your home and workplace. You feel the pressure, but this drives innovation, creativity, and curiosity. As does meeting people you never would have met before. You're being pushed to the brink, but unlike high school, you won't feel the need to ditch class. For most, once you reach higher education, you *choose* to go. Nobody is making you. So if you're pivoting in midlife and going back to school—pursuing your vision for a second career—you'll nail it because you're choosing it. For many of us, our big picture comes later in life.

My sister is a great example. She was a poor student in high school—awful, worst, terrible (love you, Sis)—and barely got through a two-year associate's nursing degree. She persisted with the nursing career, and at one point was told she had worked her way up to be a supervisor but could only assume that position if she had a legitimate degree. Here she was, a mom of three and a full-time nurse who went back to school part-time, earning straight As, because it now meant something to her. It was a part of her vision. Plus, she had figured out along the way *how she learns*. She needed this degree to arrive at her vision.

> EVERYTHING YOU'RE LEARNING AND EXPERIENCING IS A LAUNCHING PAD, NO MATTER WHAT YOU STUDY. YOUR HARD WORK IS TAKING YOUR SOMEWHERE.

I'm grateful for my degree in dentistry, but when you're young and starting out, it's not about the degree. Everything you're learning and experiencing is a launching pad, no matter what you study. Your hard work is taking your somewhere. Your emerging people skills are doing the same. You're increasing your value.

- This exercise combines the learning bucket with your *where*. Get out there and broaden your horizons! If you're seeking higher education, list three schools you're interested in that are in a new location. If that's too much of a stretch, list three courses or educational retreats that are in a different part of town. It's so important to get out of your comfort zone. If you're pursuing education at the same time, you've exponentially increased your value.

_____

_____

_____

_____

_____

THE PRICE YOU PAY COMES BACK

If you think education is expensive, try ignorance.

—ANDY MCINTYRE

I get frustrated with friends who are so concerned about the debt they've incurred. So much so, that they insist their kids should stay home instead of advancing their educations. Shockingly, I don't care how much it costs—get the hell out of the house! Go to a new city— *any* city. Go live on your own. Send your kids the message that they have to broaden their horizons. Sure, it can be daunting for a child. "Look at all the things I have to learn." Well, welcome to life.

I was never forced to learn and grow, but I immersed myself anyhow. I'd led a very sheltered life, but I was lucky as an adult to meet those mentors who informed me that there was something bigger than the four walls closing in on me. Had this not happened, I would still be living a sheltered life today. Sure, there are college degrees that are probably not the most lucrative choices to make, but even if that's your course, that college education is worth every penny. As I said, it's not about the degree.

Pursue *any* degree that lights a fire under you. Don't skate through and take the easiest major possible. That's a waste of your time. If you love English, math, history, or science, and somebody is telling you it's a foolish degree—it's not going to get you anywhere—this is not true. You love it, so it's a tremendous degree! You're fully invested, learning how to learn, and meeting new people. I promise that if your major doesn't become your career, what you achieve in terms of work ethic can be applied to any topic. Why not master something that genuinely interests you?

Following your passion will facilitate the process of understanding yourself and navigating a diverse world. You're building competence and character. Even in a small college, there will be ten times the number of people there were in high school. Believe it or not, social skills and tolerance are novel lessons that add value to anything you do. Social experiences not only provide wonderful personal lessons but also lead to advancement in the business world. When climbing any ladder in any system, learn how to be tolerant of the people above and below you, or you'll destroy your career—not because you don't have the talent or work ethic but because you won't be able to problem solve in social interactions.

Let's get into it. Student debt is good debt. It exponentially increases your value in the workforce and as a human being. I can't stand it when people argue that education is too costly. Listen, no one should walk out of undergrad owing $300 grand. No one should walk out of a professional school owing $600 grand or more. That's insane. But please, stop complaining! You can scream and yell all you want, but you won't change the mind of the university. They won't suddenly charge you 30 percent less because you think they're wrong. They're not bad or evil. All you're doing is bringing negativity into the situation when you could pour awesomeness into it.

And you're taking away from the experience.

I have dental students who have calculated how much it costs per day to learn at their clinic. "It costs X thousands of dollars to be in clinic today, and I didn't even have a patient." Well, if that's your focus, you'll never learn anything. You're not seeing that there is value added to your head each day, simply by showing up and being positive.

It's hard to hear, but nobody owes you anything. Don't look at your education as though somebody owes you something to be at the institution/course/apprenticeship. The world owes us *nothing*—nothing at all. I remember how hard I'd worked. I remember life not going my way. I needed to learn that somedays, life wasn't going to be fair and if I wanted better, I had to fight for it.

You were born valuable. People in this world innately love you, but to develop value in the *professional* world, you have to build your value consciously—focus, vision, mentors, and diverse experiences. Please don't wake up and believe that life is not a competition. Sure, that's nice to hear. But it's not true that "the pie is big enough for everybody."

The value you bring is earned through education, developing your character, and ultimately surrounding yourself with others who bring a lot of value.

- For those with student loans, don't fret! Write ten reasons why the experience was worth, or is currently worth, every penny. Never forget this.

THE VALUE YOU BRING ON

If you think it's expensive to hire a professional,
wait until you hire an amateur.

—RED ADAIR

Once you've increased your value—reached a certain level—how do you build upon it? If you want to be the leader and go-getter, understand that you might need to temporarily make less money to increase the number on your head. I'll explain. Say I'm making $1,000 an hour (this might seem like a big number from where you're at). I can increase that value by investing in others. "Anastasia is good at this, Kevin is good at that, and Mark flourishes with this." So even though I'm worth $1,000 an hour, distributing that revenue can drive my number from $1,000 to $2,000.

Too often in life, people do great things and get stuck in a number. They worry that building a team around them will either take away from their number, that their number won't grow, or they won't afford the life they want to live. They even worry that someone else on the team will outperform them. Nothing could be further from the truth. You will need to sacrifice money in the beginning. Maybe things are great, and money is flowing in, but you still have to pour a lot out the door.

Never be afraid to build a team who can outdo everything you do. No one is looking to replace you if you're a leader who has built an impressive team. They're inspired by what you've done, and everyone prospers. Building a team is a gift that many don't possess. I understand those who think they are decreasing value by hiring others. They're afraid of spending the money. They don't foresee the growth that comes from this investment.

When I have a new hire at Ignite who is doing amazing things, my value rises as a leader. I can spend my time focusing on what I'm great at instead of what I'm okay at. It's hard to accept that we're all good at only a few things. Be as good as you can be and overcome weaknesses along the way, but the moment you can unplug yourself from something you're okay at and plug in someone great, you increase your value. Ultimately, plugging others in is the super power we'll discuss next.

- Below, name three people who have increased your professional value, whether they are an educator, someone you have apprenticed, or someone you've hired.

_____

_____

_____

TAKEAWAYS

- Any form of education broadens your horizons and adds value.
- Never complain about your student loans—ever.
- Any degree you undertake will teach you how *you* learn.
- Bring on other valuable people to increase your value.
- Lose money temporarily, gain more value in the future.
- My blog, "The Value You Pay For" is found in the usual spot. The video takes a new approach to your student loan debt.

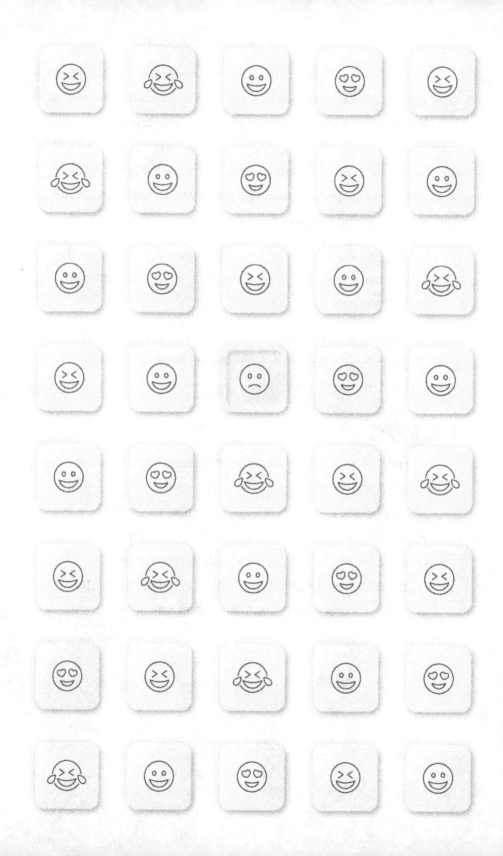

CHAPTER ELEVEN

BE A SUPERCONNECTOR

We cannot live only for ourselves. A thousand fibers connect us with our fellow men; and among those fibers, as sympathetic threads, our actions run as causes, and they come back to us as effects.

—HERMAN MELVILLE

W e each only have twenty-four hours in the day. You know that the value you bring comes from your education and experiences, but it's also profoundly impacted by the team you build around you who help scale your abilities. There's another critical element that increases the value over your head. What I've learned over the years is that my ability to connect people means that others look my way—they seek me out because I'm a superconnector.

When something comes up in my lane, I'm the right person to seek. If something comes up that's not in my lane, I can often connect two other people who can help each other. When you look at Ignite, yes, we mentor, educate, and empower people, but the reason we're sought is because others know we can connect them with armies of young dentists. Our value comes from our ability to consistently bring the right people to the right people.

> *WHAT I'VE LEARNED OVER THE YEARS IS THAT MY ABILITY TO CONNECT PEOPLE MEANS THAT OTHERS LOOK MY WAY—THEY SEEK ME OUT BECAUSE I'M A SUPERCONNECTOR.*

We spoke earlier about how one of the biggest business struggle today is that few can get a solid team to work for them—a team they can keep. Networking, meeting people, and increasing your ability to bring others together, even if it's not in your lane, is a huge win.

This book mimics the rise of your professional success. You begin with yourself. You seek *yes* and connection with others to be able to advance, until one day *you're* the one connecting others. You've reached the next level—you're the superconnector.

THE POWER OF CREATING CONNECTION

The currency of real networking is not greed but generosity.

–KEITH FERRAZZI

The group Givers Gain, founded by Dr. Ivan Misner, has chapters worldwide. They've built a network of people saying, "Our sole job is to put people from different walks of life in the same room to encourage them to help one another." I love this organization, because taking the time to connect with others teaches you how to *be* a connector—someone who helps. The reality is that the more you give, the more you'll get, and the more people will look to you as a resource. Ultimately, it *is* about who you know and what you can do for them.

Givers Gain exemplifies why networking is important. If you're starting a business or you're in a business and trying to scale, you'll need a place to go find people. It's worthwhile to attend *any* networking event and meet one person of value to you. But if you go and meet one person who connects you to ten more people, that's the person you want to know.

The goal is to reach that point where you not only know people, but also you're generous in your interactions. Others walk into the room and want to meet you. They understand that you can connect them to valuable people. They're not just meeting a nice person but someone powerful. Being a superconnector makes you a business magnet. But there's also a level of *character* that others gravitate to just for the qualities alone. The superconnector is genuinely interested and radically curious about all the people they meet—authentically wanting to *see* others, to understand them, and to help. As a result, they tend to speak less and ask more and more *questions* to find out, on a deeper level, who's in front of them. Anyone with this internal dialogue—"What can I do to help the other person?"—is extremely attractive.

We've talked about this with *The Dating Game*, but what makes us like each other initially is the genuine desire to get to know one another. On a business level, the superconnector's mystique is strong because they've learned and experienced so much and have reached such a level of success—most likely 2 percenters—that they don't need to speak to make themselves known. They're interested in others.

You can dominate any conversation by talking, but you *guide* it by asking questions and listening. And if you're also interested in helping others? Then your high status is clear.

- Think back to a networking or social event where you were talking a lot. It's okay! Write down three questions you could have asked in that moment instead of dominating the conversation.

_____

_____

_____

RECIPROCITY IS HUMAN

We make a living by what we get. We make a life by what we give.

—WINSTON CHURCHILL

Whatever you give always comes back to you, often with greater force than what you've given—every single time. In my experience, there are many times when I might want somebody's help and not mention it. I help them, and then they ask how they can reciprocate. My answer is often, "Don't worry about me right now. My goal is to help you. Let's focus on getting you from where you are to where you want to be." Then we can circle back to my goals some other time.

One, this sentiment is always appreciated because others know you're genuine. Two, it naturally inspires people to help you. Three, they probably went on to tell five other people, "You're not going to believe it. This person genuinely focused on me for nearly two hours."

Wait, what? The other person didn't want any help from you? No. There's nothing more powerful than this kind of exchange because people innately know *you're that person*. You're the person people turn to, not because of success or power but because of presence, listening, and giving—on top of everything else you've accomplished.

Always ask yourself, "Who do I want to be?" The superconnector lights up the room for two key reasons: presence and character. Are these learned or God given? Reciprocity is human, but are humans naturally prone to a grounded, giving nature? I would argue that a relatively small number are born this way. Most learn it along the way, just as you are now. Some perhaps learned these skills by watching others—like I witnessed Denny's character and leadership. Others rely on their mentors to sit them down and say, "Listen, you're coming across a little too hungry. Let me tell you a story about how to win in life." These lucky ones learn from the best of the best.

But outstanding mentorship and life experiences alone won't create this kind of character! Only a small percentage of those afforded these opportunities will *listen*. And of that small percentage, only *some* will try it out and realize the immense power that this generous, grounded, and listening approach affords. They can then reach a point where they're much more apt to openly help—because they *can*. They're not worried about putting food on the table. It's cyclical— they learn these lessons, and life goes well. And when life goes well, they know it's time to give back.

- List three superconnectors you've encountered in your life. How did their positive influence make you feel?

_____

_____

_____

_____

_____

_____

_____

_____

BECOME THE SUPERCONNECTOR TODAY

*Networking is a lot like nutrition and fitness: we know what
to do, the hard part is making it a top priority.*

—HERMINIA IBARRA

If you study super successful, happy people, you realize they're givers. They're comfortable in their own skin. They're not cocky but confident. Be this person today.

Being is different from "Fake it till you make it." Rather than faking it, you're living with intentionality on all levels. You're structuring your perfect day and sitting down with the written reminder. Put the research into your learning bucket. What are the qualities of the person you want to become? When working on yourself, create that time block in the day when you're studying what you want to achieve. Ironically, the learning bucket feeds into the personal bucket because you're creating who you are.

Some might ask themselves, "How can I be a superconnector when socializing and networking are hard?" Aside from understanding yourself, if I was sitting in front of you right now, the first question I'd ask is, "Are you where you want to be in life?" If your answer is, "No, I'd rather be here or there," I would next ask, "Can I give you a simple strategy to quickly get from where you are to where you want to be?" You'd probably say *yes*.

My response? Networking is 100 percent a part of the recipe for where you want to go.

Your ability to connect with people one-on-one, one-on-two, or one-on-three will change your landscape. If you're introverted, I understand. I used to be incredibly introverted until I got comfortable with one-on-one situations. If you sent David Rice to a networking event ten years ago, he'd walk in, and if he didn't immediately see somebody approach with a friendly face, he might roam around for five minutes and then fake a phone call.

It was truly bad. I'd sit outside thinking there was no way I could go back in. I'd leave after dressing up, driving twenty minutes, arriving, and then running out. I can't tell you how many times I used to do that because it scared the hell out of me to interact with people. I'm sure you can relate. Networking is a skill set that—like anything else—is learnable. Most aren't good at it, but if you practice walking

> NETWORKING IS 100 PERCENT A PART OF THE RECIPE FOR WHERE YOU WANT TO GO.

up to somebody new to introduce yourself—"Hey, I'm David Rice" (please use your own name)—then you're on your way to becoming a superconnector. This talent is invaluable.

Everyone at networking events is there for a reason. At one point, I learned that my job was to figure out *others'* reasons for being there, which comes full circle to the power—the presence—of listening and observation. Don't worry about going and impressing others. Don't worry about getting business from it. Just arrive and make a friend. You recall the power of not needing *yes*. Don't require anything. Introduce yourself—ask questions. People like to talk about themselves, and most in the room are searching for a friendly face and a smile. If you're ready to become the superconnector today, figure out how you can help the person in front of you, and if you can't, then who can?

When Ignite started hosting events, everyone wanted to meet me because I was the host. This phenomenon was new, but it provided a sharp learning curve toward becoming more social, a listener, and a superconnector. I ran maybe ten of these events and realized, "Wow,

I have something to offer people! They want my help as long as I keep arriving and remain open." One day, I was doing the same in rooms with one hundred people, in various cities, all the time. The attention didn't bother me anymore. I just walked in. Perhaps the confidence in knowing that I had something legitimate to offer—to help others with whatever they needed—made me feel comfortable approaching and having conversations.

If networking still frightens you, start small. Pick out scenarios that are less business driven, more socially driven, and focused on things you truly love. When broadening your horizons *and* trying to build social skills, choose groups you gravitate to because of your enthusiasm for the topic—the ultimate icebreaker. Do you love sports? Find a fan group to practice mingling. A fan of the arts? I mentioned my love for the Dalí Museum. What a fantastic way to meet people and work on my ability to open up! As an introvert, you still might feel a bit awkward, but you're in a comfort zone regarding interest. If you're an extrovert, these get-togethers are an opportunity to practice listening.

My wife is an introvert. She doesn't like social situations. Often my advice to her looks like this: "Anastasia, first of all, you must realize that people are just people. They're not doing you a favor by coming over and having a conversation with you. You don't need to feel humbled and say, 'Thank you so much!' We're all just people. Go to an event, be you, and stay interested in others. From there, it's just repetition and understanding that the first few times might not go so well. One day, it will be easier. You'll naturally be friendly, interested, and engaged. Keep doing it. By the fifth, sixth, or seventh time, you'll gauge uncomfortable situations that have *nothing to do with you.*"

Sometimes, it's not you. It's the wrong room. Move on.

Confidence—the humbled, inquisitive nature of the superconnector—develops by pushing through discomfort. It's the same with public speaking. I was petrified of speaking and now I love it, but that didn't happen overnight. I'm a huge fan of the Myers–Briggs Type Indicator and DISC personality tests. You can easily find them online. These give you a great snapshot of where you're at concerning a number of characteristics, but no person is set in stone. I've become a driver and influencer over time—which was not my personality growing up—but by implementing this work, I've evolved. Your personality will shift throughout this process.

Many are timid, thinking the world has all the power over them. That was me in a nutshell. But you *can* learn to stand firm. You can practice presence of character—just like anything else. It's a process. If you need to increase your social skills to move ahead, then network! Seek out a 2 percenter who is already socially excellent. This goes for friendship as well. If you're introverted to a fault, find those extroverted friends and mentors who can show you a different approach.

- Take the Myers–Briggs Type Indicator and DISC personality tests and write your results below. Five years from now, do it again.

_____

_____

_____

_____

_____

_____

_____

_____

_____

_____

_____

GENUINE CONNECTION COMES FROM BEING YOU

Once I began to realize that there were no rules and that my path didn't have to look like everyone else's, I relaxed and my whole world opened up.

—G. BRIAN BENSON

Preparing for a social event can be stressful. We all walk into our closets and have that moment when we tell ourselves, "That's the outfit. I feel better when I'm in it." So that's the one you need to wear. Do your hair the way it needs to be done and crank the music the way it needs to be cranked. Get into your zone before you go off on your way. Have your process for getting ready, and one day you'll wake up and say to yourself, "I'm looking forward to this event. Meeting people is no longer stressful."

There's a charisma to those who are comfortable in their own skin, and it's the hallmark of a superconnector—someone relaxed enough to engage and connect with others.

Learning and working to be comfortable in your own skin bring wisdom and humility. It can be dangerous for those who are born to do it. They get cocky and make it all about them. You know the type: they don't listen, and they talk too much. We need both extroverts and introverts in this world, but introverts enjoy a massive win because they're inherently listeners. Those who want to learn about others are at a considerable advantage. They have a talent extroverts need to improve upon. But build that confidence, introverts!

After the Myers–Briggs and DISC assessments, ask yourself, "Do I think I have control in the world?" and "Do I *not* feel like I have control in the world?" and "Am I task driven?" and "Am I people driven?" The answers highlight your strengths, so that you better understand your weaknesses. As I said, this work *will* shift your personality over time. I'm more myself today, leading the Ignite team, than I was heading my twenty-year dental practice.

Why did I feel like something was missing all those years ago, as I sat in front of Lake Eerie? There was a time when I was a version of David Rice that I didn't like. I was someone who I didn't want to be. It was a gut instinct that told me I was on the wrong path. I could have learned these truths sooner, but I discovered it all the hard way. I should have read this book years ago! It would have taught me that I'm more in control of my destiny than I initially thought possible. You are as well.

TAKEAWAYS

- Talk if you want to dominate a conversation. Listen if you want to guide it.
- Networking is hard for everyone. Keep practicing.
- Superconnectors are innately genuine, curious, and helpful.
- Be the person you wish to be today—don't fake it.
- Learn more "Tips for Becoming a Superconnector" at drdavidrice. com/resources and watch my video to delve deeper into the power of connection.

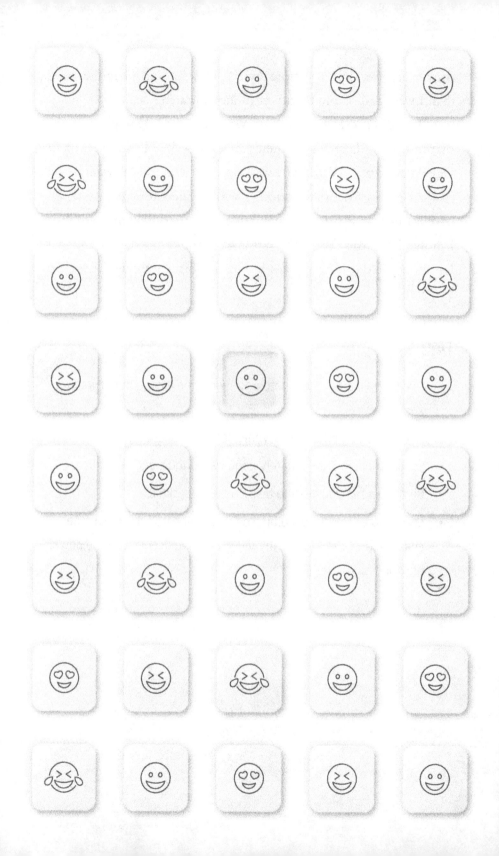

CHAPTER TWELVE

TAKE CONTROL OF YOUR FUTURE

Weakness of attitude becomes weakness of character.

—ALBERT EINSTEIN

A t the heart of it all, attitude is destiny. It's easy to spot great attitudes in others—at any restaurant, at any store, or just walking down the street. People with positive demeanors attract others. You want to be around them and to put it into social media terms: "Likes like likes." If you have a team of people with great attitudes, it's almost guaranteed that they have a circle of friends with the same outlook. These are the individuals you want to be around.

At Ignite, we hire for attitude over aptitude. Those joining us can learn along the way because our collective enthusiasm funnels into new hires. I've met all these dental students at different phases who truly desired to be better. In fact, they wanted better for the whole profession. These young professionals—with incredible attitudes and work ethics—now lead our team in different divisions. They're also finding younger people who say to themselves, "I want to grow up to be like them because they're just starting out. And look at how quickly they're advancing. They're different from anyone else our age."

Step into any position, life change, or new challenge with a great attitude, and you will succeed and inspire others—the energy self-perpetuates.

Coming full circle—when you've found your *where*, *what*, and *why*, you have a solid attitude because you're ultimately seeking happiness. When you have someone negative in your life—I don't care if it's your mother, father, brother, or sister—you create boundaries. Surround yourself with positive, uplifting people. Your positive attitude is a direct exception of the work you're doing.

> STEP INTO ANY POSITION, LIFE CHANGE, OR NEW CHALLENGE WITH A GREAT ATTITUDE, AND YOU WILL SUCCEED AND INSPIRE OTHERS— THE ENERGY SELF-PERPETUATES.

I'll clarify this idea with a story that you might relate to. I spoke about *pessimism* at a speaking engagement, and a respected colleague responded, "I have to challenge you on the pessimism. A lot of research shows that we're either born optimistic or pessimistic."

I stopped, smiled, and replied, "You sound like a guy who thinks I believe you're a pessimist. I don't at all. You're a contrarian. You're one of the three people I need."

I already knew him, and he was the kind of guy who could see what I couldn't. He's very analytical, does the research, and checks all the boxes. As you know, that's not me. And that's why I'm attracted to his personality. Saying all this to him put a big smile on his face.

Listen, life is hard, and we all have different perspectives. The can-do attitude comes from putting in the work. Just because you were born a pessimist doesn't mean you can't work on yourself and improve. You might lean a certain way, but you can learn to be better. You can learn how—in the company of others—to consciously choose to check that pessimism and bring something different.

Most would never know it, but behind closed doors, I'm a skeptic. I'm looking for the flaw. That's just me, but I don't show that side of myself to others. I've learned there's a place where it serves me, but in most instances, it doesn't serve me well. You don't have to be born with a happy-go-lucky attitude, but working on your attitude will benefit your future.

The guy who worried he was a pessimist is a great example of how we compartmentalize ourselves. After that speaking engagement, I tested things out a few hours later by sitting and talking with him in a different environment. As it turns out, he's a wristwatch guy. I had a theory kicking around in my head, so I inquired, "Tell me about your watches." He instantly glowed and told me he had some videos but was afraid he was being too braggadocious. I insisted on seeing the videos and then witnessed the *optimist*—proud to show his watch safe that self-winds all the timepieces. The expression on his face totally changed when he was in his element.

We all have about three of these golden veins of optimism. Understanding what makes us light up can help bring our optimism forward and check pessimism when necessary.

- Self-awareness is the gateway to a positive attitude—it's the door to everything you wish to achieve in life. Write three things in your life that effortlessly make you glow.

_____

_____

_____

MAKE IT HAPPEN NOW

To be empowered is to move through the world without fear or apology, and with these gifts, come an even deeper privilege—the ability to take charge of your own life and claim your rights.

—OPRAH WINFREY

I warned you before that we're not pulling punches here, and I meant it. So let's explore the *make-it-happen* attitude versus the victim mentality. How many reasons have we heard why somebody can't do something—because of where they grew up, their family dynamic, or what they didn't have opportunity-wise? Listen, there are those on this earth who *are* victims. In some parts of the world, people simply try to wake up tomorrow morning, not knowing if they'll have food or shelter. They worry their belongings will be destroyed by war. That's a victim.

It might anger you, but no one in the United States of America is a victim—unless you choose it. Yes, you may have extreme hardship. However, history shows that some of the most successful, impactful, and influential people on this earth overcame adversity. Separating yourself from the victim mindset comes down to these critical questions: "How do I get out? How do I get better? Who do I need around me to help me do it?" What you've gone through in no way sets you back. It puts you at an advantage.

Oprah Winfrey is a great example. Actress Viola Davis appeared on her show. I watched in awe. These two women came from unimaginable hardship. Their success arose from their ability to affirm, "You know what I'm not going to stand for? *Failing.* I'm going to win. I will overcome. As hard as it is, I will work harder. As awful as it is, I seek the opposite of my former environment so that my kids, family, and life never have to be like this again."

The victim mindset experiences hardship and folds, where the winner decides to do better for themselves—embracing whatever it takes to overcome. Respectfully, this is an easier path for some than others, but no matter what you've been through, you can achieve success when you use your struggles to propel you. A victim gives up. They play that card as an excuse, compared to someone who's endured the same hardship and won't back down.

Harsh, I know—and I'll preface it with the fact that I'm a white man. No matter my obstacles, life is still easier for me. I realized this as an adult. When I was young and paying for my education, I didn't know my path was easier. But Winfrey and Davis are vastly more successful than I could ever dream of being, and they had far more challenging obstacles. So everything is possible. Allow your struggles in life to enhance and add more meaning to the work you're doing.

> A WIN COMES FROM SIMPLY MOVING CLOSER TO WHAT YOU WANT. YOU'RE ON THE PATH YOU'VE CHOSEN. YOU HAVE MOMENTUM.

This process is already a win for you, no matter your background, where you want to go, or how fast you hope to get there. The common proverb, "It's not the destination; it's the journey," holds meaning. A win comes from simply moving closer to what you want. You're on the path you've chosen. You have momentum. There's a snowball effect—you're working toward your big picture, surrounding yourself with the right people, and because of this, your happiness and attitude skyrocket—you're positioning yourself for success.

People who strive for something better stand out. I see it all the time. As for those who approach me to ask questions—even if they're not at the stage of seeking help or mentorship—I know they're going somewhere because they just keep showing up, even when it's hard for them. It's common for successful individuals to say, "I remember being that quiet person in the back of the room—afraid to ask." People are afraid their questions are dumb or that they're asking about something they should already know.

Two percenters were timid at one point. But we (leaders) see you (the future) showing up in the back of the room every time. We see you *more* if you're in the front asking questions. Being present is an incredible indicator of attitude—of someone making a dream happen for themselves. We're in an era where you don't have to be physically present to gain access to several different rooms, but keep in mind that being on a screen doesn't mask attitude or character. It amplifies it.

At Ignite, we're strategically looking for character, attitude, and those who consistently show up. On the other hand, we meet many that I cross off the list. If they ever ask me for something, the answer will be *no*, because they expressed interest and *didn't show up.* They scheduled a meeting and were twenty minutes late. They didn't have anything to offer but thought they did. In many ways, this era high-lights character more clearly than any other. Showing up with that can-do attitude will get you through the door and beyond.

- List three hardships you've faced in life. This might be difficult but take a moment and consider how you can own these experiences instead of allowing them to set you back.

_____

_____

_____

_____

_____

A SYSTEM FOR SUCCESS

Being busy does not always mean real work. The object of all work is production or accomplishment and to either of these ends there must be forethought, system, planning, intelligence, and honest purpose, as well as perspiration. Seeming to do is not doing.

—THOMAS A. EDISON

You're better equipped for hardship—past or present—when you've built a system for success. Humans are innately important, but 94 percent of our success is systems based. When you have a methodology, there's something to lean on. When you've invested time in your vision, there's a bedrock to help you remember *why* all this is important in the first place. You find your mentors—minimally three—but if you can get two of each, great. In essence, you have a team supporting you.

There are millions of people out there who have a great idea or aspiration for their lives, but only a small percentage actually do something about it.

Any system for success will involve many people. The power of *who* can make or break your ability to venture into the unknown. Let's get practical. Everyone needs a financial planner, no matter who you are. You need a great accountant, whether you think you do or not. These are definitive team members. At some point, you might need a great attorney. Make a short list of professionals. Also include a doctor, therapist, or spiritual coach.

There's no end to the number of specialists who can help you on this path. If you're looking for something easier, there are countless apps these days to assist you without needing to be one-on-one. Perhaps you'd benefit from a fitness/nutrition app, a focus or meditation app, or an app tracking your sleep. You can't have clarity of vision when running on four hours of sleep! You think you can, but no human *actually* can.

Getting all these lifestyle support systems in place is essential. Do it early.

Apps are great because they allow you to measure things—physically, mentally, financially, and also in terms of productivity. Measurement is crucial. We need it. What is the measure of success? It's not *all* about the numbers, but you get to a point when you realize, "It *is* kind of about the numbers." The numbers matter.

Indulge me while I share this hard truth: you're selling yourself in this life. No, I'm not referring to the traditional sense of "selling out," but understand the value on your head. You are selling your abilities and character. What you bring to the table is influenced by what's happening in the background—your planning, well-being, mental health, and relationships.

You've come this far and might be wondering what the next steps are. I have several to offer, but let's start with this: *sell what you have to offer with confidence.* You're in a solid position to land that next job or pitch that idea for a company. You're evolving and ready to put yourself out there. Looking at this from a different angle. People buy what you have to give. They're also *investing* in you when your character, determination, and attitude shine through.

What you've studied in these twelve chapters isn't the tip of the iceberg—it's the portion below the sea. You're building your infrastructure. Moving ahead, you're ready for that magnificent iceberg to crest the waves.

You might be asking yourself, "Okay, but what's the next *strategic* step?" Follow this system. It powers you through hard times and leads you to joyous moments of personal discovery. Life happens. It happens all the time, but what you are now accomplishing will prevent you from ever being stuck again. You have daily milestones, a structure for your perfect day, and a bucket method balancing your priorities. This structure guarantees that you're moving toward your big picture *every single day.*

This is a lot to digest but consider this *lifetime* work. You don't have to reach your goal today. Keep plugging away at it for a better tomorrow. Go one bite at a time. Get a little better. Everyone can.

I promise that this vision for yourself is possible. You are in control of your future. No, it's not a cakewalk. The happiness and fulfillment you feel showing up for your big picture each day? These emotions *draw success to you* because you're on your path, and you understand yourself and the potential for your life. You accept *yes* or *no* because what others say doesn't matter. You're showing up for your day with purpose and waking up each morning knowing that it all has meaning.

You're becoming what you were meant to be.

- Write the most impactful idea this book has left you with and how you plan to take action with that aha moment.

TAKEAWAYS

- Attitude is destiny.

- Don't allow hardships to hold you back.

- What you're building is a system for success that you can lean on.

- Make a list of professionals you need on your team—do it early.

- Apps are a great tool to manage your life and receive data on your progress.

- "Your Future—Be the Driver," will get you into the driver's seat. Head back over to drdavidrice.com/resources or snap the QR code at the end of the book.

CONCLUSION

*Few people attain great lives, in large part because
it is just so easy to settle for a good life.*

—JIM COLLINS

It's easy to fall into a space where life is just happening. This isn't a shameful approach, but in truth, before you know it, five years have gone by, and you can't get that lost time back. The habits that you've formed become difficult to break. When you start early with the *right* habits, you put yourself on the path to what you want.

Coming out of school, you're used to living lean—a regimented lifestyle—because there's a class schedule, you're on the low end of the totem pole, and you're going *all in* on everything. You give, give, and give! When you don't have enough time or money, you get trapped there—you stay in your comfort zone instead of getting *uncomfortable*.

The reality is that, to grow, you have to be uncomfortable. Unless you inherit money or win the lottery, which probably wouldn't make you happy anyway, there is inherent discomfort in building a business or jumping five rungs up the ladder. That's how it works. When you're starting out and used to playing by the rules, it's easy to stay in a place that is familiar—and suffocating.

Keep pushing ahead and think out of the box! Live lean while you're working toward the future you want. Don't settle. Yes, no one wants to be uncomfortable, but you're alive! To keep that vitality strong, don't settle for what others tell you is a good life. Always know that you desire something bigger. The human mind dreams big for a reason. We're meant to achieve remarkable things, so don't let your past or derailed ideas about the future set you back. The time to begin this work is now. You have nothing to lose and everything to gain when you invest in yourself and your potential, each and every day.

As you now know, it's easy to habitually do what parents, friends, or anyone else has done. It's hard to break free into your own vision. I've noticed that there are two stages when you can launch: when you first come out of the gate, or when you wake up one day and the pain's just so bad that you can't stand it anymore, and you have to make a shift. That was me. It doesn't have to be you.

I'm a huge fan of Brendon Burchard. What I continue to learn from him is that unless you're focused, dialed in, and taking comfort in being uncomfortable, there's no growth. One of his marketing principles instructs us to either focus on beginners or experts and never on anyone in the middle, because they're lost. This mentality applies to what you're doing.

Dial in at the start, or you'll get to that point where you coast, never change, or wake up one day and need some *radical* change. Start this work today, and you'll have no regrets. If you finished reading this book at forty, fifty, or beyond, you'll inherently know that you have to go *all in* on this, or you're destined to keep the unfulfilling routine. And if you're a reader in this group, I'm so excited for you.

My friends, you've come so far. Will you put in the work? What will you do *right now*? Your life, dreams, and big picture are so precious. I want this level of success for you—for your vision to come to life. You've already proved your willingness to tackle the deeper work, but that was just preparation.

This book is coming to an end, but I'd argue that once you've absorbed this new information, it's only the beginning for you. You're the kind of person who shows up, and now I want you to put this into action. I believe in you, but more importantly, you need to believe in yourself—you need to do the work.

Here are your next steps:

1. COMPLETE ANY EXERCISES YOU'VE MISSED. WRITE IT ALL DOWN.

2. REVIEW THE BLOGS AND VIDEOS FOR EACH CORRESPONDING CHAPTER.

3. MOST IMPORTANTLY, USE MY TWELVE-WEEK CALENDAR MOVING FORWARD.

At this point, you're already a part of a small percentage of the population. Here's the hard truth: research has predicted only 8 percent of people achieve their goals.[9] Now, the question is will you be one of this small percentage who takes action and does something with what you've learned?

I get it if you're not steering the ship after years of drifting but ready for a change. That was me. I got so comfortable that I couldn't stand it one more day. Are you there now? Are you in that place? If

---

9   Marcel Schwantes, "Science Says Only 8 Percent of People Actually Achieve Their Goals. Here Are 7 Things They Do Differently," Inc., https://www.inc.com/marcel-schwantes/science-says-only-8-percent-of-people-actually-achieve-their-goals-here-are-7-things-they-do-differently.html.

you're ready, keep working on these principles. If not, shelf this book and pull it out again.

I encourage you to dive in at the pace that works for you. It's hard to shift your life when things are going *pretty good* because many fear there's too much to lose if they stop doing their day-to-day routine. You have more to lose when you don't lean into the discomfort of change—change that is calling out to you.

Human nature is stubborn. You have a heart attack before eating right and exercising. You feel depression and hopelessness before you leave a bad situation. I'm not repeating myself; I'm driving it into your head. Start this work early, and if pivoting, know that there's a wealth of potential in front of you. It's never too late.

> YOU HAVE MORE TO LOSE WHEN YOU DON'T LEAN INTO THE DISCOMFORT OF CHANGE—CHANGE THAT IS CALLING OUT TO YOU.

As we sum everything up, I have a tool that will carry this focus through the next twelve weeks. You've envisioned your blocks, but let's put them into action. As always, use a pencil because things shift. Each PDF will inspire you to focus on one chapter at a time—reminding you of your core values, buckets, and perfect day. There's no need to be an expert at scheduling right now. You're building a muscle while also allowing the information in this book to process.

I want to thank you for coming on this journey. I believe in you, and I'm proud of what you've accomplished so far. Work through these next twelve weeks and deepen what you already understand about yourself. Consider this a lifestyle. As you consciously change your world, the world around you changes. That's the funny thing about life—it responds to your efforts and actions. One thing builds upon the next. You find yourself achieving what you only dreamed of—your impossible.

Here's my last thought: make yourself happy. Society wants you to believe that being comfortable is a happy place—that being at leisure is a sign of happiness. It isn't. Achieving your goals and reaching new heights will fill you with energy and joy while attracting those into your life who are also striving to be their best. Understand that you're building your purpose. It will look different for everyone, but ultimately *purpose* is the fuel that propels you through your perfect day with meaning, focus, and joy—with a system to hold it all together.

Here's your system for the next twelve weeks. You're well on your way. Keep going.

Go to drdavidrice.com/resources or use the QR code for the twelve-page PDF download. Print it. Use it! It will change your life.